C. K. WILLIAMS

SELECTED POEMS

Farrar, Straus and Giroux

New York

Library of Congress Cataloging-in-Publication Data
Williams, C. K. (Charles Kenneth), 1936–
[Poems. Selections]
Selected poems / C. K. Williams.
p.   cm.
Includes index
I. Title.
PS3573.I4483A6   1994   811'.54—dc20   94-14359   CIP

Poems in the section entitled "New Poems" have appeared in the
following publications: "Hercules, Deianira, Nessus" in The Times
Literary Supplement; "Dominion: Depression" in Library Chronicle;
"My Fly," "Thirst," and "Villanelle of the Suicide's Mother" in The
New Yorker; "Secrets" in Antaeus; "Spider Psyche" and "My Book, My
Book" in the New England Review; and "Interrogation II" in
Transforming Vision: Writers on Art (The Art Institute of Chicago/The
Bulfinch Press, 1994).

Contents

FROM *Lies* [1969]

FROM *I Am the Bitter Name* [1972]

FROM *Flesh and Blood* [1987]

FROM *A Dream of Mind* [1992]

New Poems

Lies

[1 9 6 9]

A Day for Anne Frank

1

I look onto an alley here
where, though tough weeds and flowers thrust up
through cracks and strain
toward the dulled sunlight,
there is the usual filth spilling from cans,
the heavy soot shifting in the gutters.
People come by mostly
to walk their dogs or take the shortcut
between the roaring main streets,
or just to walk
and stare up at the smoky windows,
but this morning when I looked out
children were there running back and forth
between the houses toward me.
They were playing with turtles—
skimming them down the street
like pennies or flat stones,
and bolting, shouting, after the broken corpses.
One had a harmonica, and as he ran,
his cheeks bloating and collapsing like a heart,
I could hear its bleat, and then the girls' screams
suspended behind them with their hair,
and all of them: their hard, young breath,
their feet pounding wildly on the pavement to the corner.

2

I thought of you at that age.
Little Sister, I thought of you,
thin as a door,
and of how your thighs would have swelled

3

and softened like cake,
your breasts have bleached
and the new hair growing on you like song
would have stiffened and gone dark.
There was rain for a while, and then not.
Because no one came, I slept again,
and dreamed that you were here with me,
snarled on me like wire,
tangled so closely to me that we were vines
or underbrush together,
or hands clenched.

3

They are cutting babies in half on bets.
The beautiful sergeant has enough money to drink
for a week.
The beautiful lieutenant can't stop betting.
The little boy whimpers
he'll be good.
The beautiful cook is gathering up meat
for the dogs.
The beautiful dogs
love it all.
Their flanks glisten.
They curl up in their warm kennels
and breathe.
They breathe.

4

Little Sister,
you are a clot
in the snow,
blackened,
a chunk of phlegm
or puke

and there are men with faces
leaning over you with watercans

watering you!
in the snow, as though flowers would sprout
from your armpits
and genitals.

Little Sister,
I am afraid of the flowers sprouting from you

I am afraid of the silver petals
that crackle
of the stems darting
in the wind
of the roots

5

The twilight rots.
Over the greasy bridges and factories,
it dissolves
and the clouds swamp in its rose
to nothing.
I think sometimes the slag heaps by the river
should be bodies
and that the pods of moral terror
men make of their flesh should split
and foam their cold, sterile seeds into the tides
like snow
or ash.

6

Stacks of hair were there
little mountains
the gestapo children must have played in

and made love in and loved
the way children love haystacks or mountains

O God the stink
of hair oil and dandruff

their mothers must have thrown them into their tubs
like puppies and sent them to bed

coming home so filthy stinking

of jew's hair

of gold fillings, of eyelids

7

Under me on a roof
a sparrow little by little
is being blown away.
A cage of bone is left,
part of its wings,
a stain.

8

And in Germany the streetcar conductors go to work
in their stiff hats,
depositing workers and housewives
where they belong,
pulling the bell chains,
moving drive levers forward or back.

9

I am saying goodbye to you before our death. Dear Father:
I am saying goodbye to you before my death. We are so

anxious to live, but all is lost—we are not allowed! I am so
afraid of this death, because little children are thrown into
graves alive. Goodbye forever.
I kiss you.

10

Come with me Anne.
Come,
it is awful not to be anywhere at all,
to have no one
like an old whore,
a general.

Come sit with me here
kiss me; my heart too is wounded
with forgiveness.

There is an end now.
Stay.
Your foot hooked through mine
your hand against my hand
your hip touching me lightly

it will end now
it will not begin again

Stay
they will pass
and not know us

the cold brute earth
is asleep

there is no danger

there is nothing

Anne

there is nothing

Even If I Could

Except for the little girl
making faces behind me, and the rainbow
behind her, and the school and the truck,
the only thing between you
and infinity
is me. Which is why you cover your ears
when I speak and why
you're always oozing around the edges,
clinging, trying
to go by me.

And except for my eyes and the back
of my skull, and then my hair,
the wall, the concrete
and the fire-cloud, except for them
you would see
God. And that's why rage howls in your arms
like a baby and why I can't move—
because of the thunder and the shadows
merging like oil and the smile gleaming
through the petals.

Let me tell you how sick with loneliness
I am. What can I do while the distance
throbs on my back like a hump,
or say, with stars stinging me
through the wheel? You are before me,
behind me things rattle their deaths out
like paper. The angels ride
in their soft saddles:
except for them, I would come closer
and go.

Saint Sex

there are people whose sex
keeps growing even when they're old whose
genitals swell like tumors endlessly
until they are all sex and nothing else nothing
that moves or thinks nothing
but great inward and outward handfuls of gristle

think of them men
who ooze their penises out like snail
feet whose testicles clang in their scrotums women
are like anvils to them the world an
anvil they want to take whole buildings
in their arms they want
to come in the windows to run antennas
through their ducts like ramrods and women
these poor women who dream and dream of
the flower they can't sniff it sends buds
into their brain they feel their neural
river clot with moist fingers the ganglia
hardening like ant eggs the ends
burning off

pity them these people there are no wars
for them there is no news no
summer no reason they are so humble they want
nothing they have no hands or faces
pity them at night whispering I love
you to themselves and during the day how they
walk along smiling and suffering pity
them love them they are
angels

Loss

In this day and age Lord
you are like one of those poor farmers
who burns the forests off
and murders his land and then
can't leave and goes sullen and lean
among the rusting yard junk, the scrub
and the famished stock.

Lord I have felt myself raked
into the earth like manure,
harrowed and plowed under,
but I am still enough like you
to stand on the porch
chewing a stalk or drinking
while tall weeds come up dead
and the house dogs, snapping
their chains like moths, howl
and point towards the withering
meadows at nothing.

The World's Greatest Tricycle-Rider

The world's greatest tricycle-rider
is in my heart, riding like a wildman,
no hands, almost upside down along
the walls and over the high curbs
and stoops, his bell rapid firing,
the sun spinning in his spokes like a flame.

But he is growing older. His feet
overshoot the pedals. His teeth set
too hard against the jolts, and I am afraid
that what I've kept from him is what
tightens his fingers on the rubber grips
and drives him again and again on the same block.

Dimensions

There is a world somewhere else that is unendurable.
Those who live in it are helpless in the hands of elements,
they are like branches in the deep woods in wind
that whip their leaves off and slice the heart of the night
and sob. They are like boats bleating wearily in fog.

But here, no matter what, we know where we stand.
We know more or less what comes next. We hold out.
Sometimes a dream will shake us like little dogs, a fever
hang on so we're not ourselves or love wring us out,
but we prevail, we certify and make sure, we go on.

There is a world that uses its soldiers and widows
for flour, its orphans for building stone, its legs for pens.
In that place, eyes are softened and harmless like God's
and all blend in the traffic of their tragedy and pass by
like people. And sometimes one of us, losing the way,
will drift over the border and see them there, dying,
laughing, being revived. When we come home, we are halfway.
Our screams heal the torn silence. We are the scars.

Hood

Remember me? I was the one
in high school you were always afraid of.
I kept cigarettes in my sleeve, wore
engineer's boots, long hair, my collar
up in back and there were always
girls with me in the hallways.

You were nothing. I had it in for you—
when I peeled rubber at the lights
you cringed like a teacher.
And when I crashed and broke both lungs
on the wheel, you were so relieved
that you stroked the hard Ford paint
like a breast and your hands shook.

It Is This Way with Men

They are pounded into the earth
like nails; move an inch,
they are driven down again.
The earth is sore with them.
It is a spiny fruit
that has lost hope
of being raised and eaten.
It can only ripen and ripen.
And men, they too are wounded.
They too are sifted from their loss
and are without hope. The core
softens. The pure flesh softens
and melts. There are thorns, there
are the dark seeds, and they end.

Of What Is Past

I hook my fingers into the old tennis court fence
and kneel down in an overgrowth of sharp weeds
to watch the troopers in their spare compound drill.

Do you remember when this was a park? When girls
swung their rackets here in the hot summer mornings
and came at night to open their bodies to us?

Now gun-butts stamp the pale clay like hooves.
Hard boots gleam.
And still, children play tag and hide-and-seek

beyond the barriers. Lovers sag in the brush.
It's not them, it's us: we know too much.
Soon only the past will know what we know.

Being Alone

Never on one single pore Eternity
have I been touched by your snows

or felt your shy mouth tremble,
your breath break on me

like the white wave. I have not felt
your nakedness tear me

with hunger or your silver hands
betray me but today I promise

whatever flower of your house
should bloom I will stay

locked to its breast.
Like little fish who live

harmlessly under the bellies of sharks,
I will go where you go,

drift inconspicuously
in the raw dredge of your power

like a leaf, a bubble of carrion,
a man who has understood and does not.

Giving It Up

It is an age
of such bestial death
that even before we die
our ghosts go.
I have felt mine while I slept
send shoots over my face,
probing some future char
there, tasting the flesh
and the sweat
as though for the last time.

And I have felt him
extricate himself and go,
crying, softening himself
and matching his shape
to new bodies; merging,
sliding into souls,
into motors, buildings,
stop signs, policemen—
anything.

By morning, he is back.
Diminished, shorn
of his light, he lies crumpled
in my palm, shivering
under my breath like cellophane.
And every day
there is nothing to do
but swallow him like a cold
tear
and get on with it.

For Gail, When I Was Five

My soul is out back eating your soul.
I have you tied in threads like a spider
and I am drinking down your laughter
in huge spoonfuls. It is like tinsel.
It sprays over the crusty peach baskets
and the spades hung on pegs. It is like air
and you are screaming, or I am, and we are
in different places with wild animal faces.

What does God do to children who touch
in the darkness of their bodies and laugh?
What does he think of little underpants
that drift down on the hose like flowers?
God eats your soul, like me. He drinks
your laughter. It is God in the history
of my body who melts your laughter
and spits it in the wounds of my life like tears.

Ten Below

It's bad enough crying for children
suffering neglect and starvation in our world
without having on a day like this
to see an old cart horse covered with foam,
quivering so hard that when he stops
the wheels still rock slowly in place
like gears in an engine.
A man will do that, shiver where he stands,
frozen with false starts,
just staring,
but with a man you can take his arm,
talk him out of it, lead him away.

What do you do when both hands
and your voice are simply goads?
When the eyes you solace see space,
the wall behind you, the wisp of grass
pushing up through the curb at your feet?
I have thought that all the animals
we kill and maim, if they wanted to
could stare us down, wither us
and turn us to smoke with their glances—
they forbear because they pity us,
like angels, and love of something else
is why they suffer us and submit.

But this is Pine Street, Philadelphia, 1965.
You don't believe
in anything divine being here.
There is an old plug with a worn blanket
thrown on its haunches. There is a wagon
full of junk—pipes and rotted sinks,
the grates from furnaces—and there
is a child walking beside the horse

with sugar, and the mammoth head lowering,
delicately nibbling from those vulnerable
fingers. You can't cut your heart out.
Sometimes, just what is, is enough.

Downwards

This is the last day of the world. On the river docks
I watch for the last time the tide get higher
and chop in under the stinking pilings. How the small creatures
who drift dreaming of hands and lungs must sting,
rotting alive in the waste spill, coming up dead
with puffy stomachs paler than the sky or faces.
There is deep fire fuming ash to the surface.
It is the last tide and the last evening and from now
things will strive back downwards.
A fish thrown up will gasp in the flare
and flop back hopelessly through the mud flats to the water.
The last man, an empty bottle with no message, is here, is me,
and I am rolling, fragile as a bubble in the upstream spin,
battered by carcasses, drawn down by the lips of weeds
to the terrible womb of torn tires and children's plastic shoes
and pennies and urine. I am no more, and what is left,
baled softly with wire, floating
like a dark pillow in the hold of the brown ship, is nothing.
It dreams. Touching fangs delicately with cranes
and forklifts, it rests silently in its heavy ripening.
It stands still on the water, rocking, blinking.

Halves

I am going to rip myself down the middle into two pieces
because there is something in me that is neither
the right half nor the left half nor between them.
It is what I see when I close my eyes, and what I see.

As in this room there is something neither ceiling
nor floor, not space, light, heat or even
the deep skies of pictures, but something that beats softly
against others when they're here and others not here,

that leans on me like a woman,
curls up in my lap and walks
with me to the kitchen or out of the house altogether
to the street—I don't feel it, but it beats and beats;

so my life: there is this, neither before me
nor after, not up, down, backwards nor forwards from me.
It is like the dense, sensory petals in a breast
that sway and touch back. It is like the mouth of a season,

the cool speculations bricks murmur, the shriek in orange,
and though it is neither true nor false, it tells me
that it is quietly here, and, like a creature, is in pain;
that when I ripen it will crack open the locks, it will love me.

FROM

I Am the Bitter Name

[1 9 7 2]

I Am the Bitter Name

And Abraham said to him, "And art thou, indeed,
he that is called Death?"
He answered, and said, "I am the Bitter Name."

the little children have been fighting
a long long time for their beloved country
their faces are hardening like meat
left out their bodies squashed flat
like flowers in lawbooks don't fit
with the keys to eternal sorrow anymore
is the best toy always death? everyone
crying in the sleepy hair inexhaustible
agony in the dark cups of the skull
unquenchable agony your hands shriek
on my spine like locked brakes in
the torn nostrils tendrils in the mouth
vines the little soldiers play
wounding the little generals play hurt
forever they sharpen things they put
things in things they pull them out
will you make freedom for me? in
the cheekbone fire in the lips my
justice is to forget being here my liberty
wanting to hate them how they are shipped
home in ice-cream bags and being able to

The Spirit the Triumph

do you remember learning to tie your shoes?
astonishing! the loops you had to make the delicate
adjustments the pulling-through tightening impossible!
the things we learn!
putting a bridle on a horse when he's head-shy
getting your hands under a girl's sweater
no wonder we are the crown of all that exists
we can do anything how we climb chimneys
how we put one foot on the gas one on the clutch
and make the car go nothing too difficult nothing!

crutches artificial arms have you seen that?
how they pick their cups up and use razors? amazing!
and the wives shine it for them at night
they're sleeping the wives take it out of the room
and polish it with its own special rag
it's late they hold it against their bellies
the leather laces dangle into their laps
the mechanisms slip noiselessly
lowering the hook softly onto their breasts
we men! aren't we something? I mean
we are worth thinking about aren't we?
we are the end we are the living end

Clay out of Silence

chances are we will sink quietly back
into oblivion without a ripple
we will go back into the face
down through the mortars as though it hadn't happened

earth: I'll remember you
you were the mother you made pain
I'll grind my thorax against you for the last time
and put my hand on you again to comfort you

sky: could we forget?
we were the same as you were
we couldn't wait to get back sleeping
we'd have done anything to be sleeping

and trees angels for being thrust up here
and stones for cracking in my bare hands
because you foreknew
there was no vengeance for being here

when we were flesh we were eaten
when we were metal we were burned back
there was no death anywhere but now
when we were men when we became it

Flat

the pillows are going insane
they are like shells the skulls have risen out of them like locusts
leaving faces in them but cold vacant immobile
heavy with tears
they are like clouds and are so sick of us
so furious with us they swear next time
when we come back if they can they will spring up and our faces will
     empty
next time they will soar like clouds and dissolve
and not touch us it is morning
our heads thrown back in agony

the pillows are going insane
from the grief of being laid down
and having to stare unquestioningly like flowers
and be in all places like flowers each man one in his house
one in his barracks in his jail cell
they swear if they weren't going insane they would call to each other
like flowers and spring up and come closer
but they must stay quietly
they must have faces like men and wait like men
the dead casings the filling and emptying going insane

The Beginning of April

I feel terribly strong today
it's like the time I arm-wrestled a friend
and beat him so badly I sprained his wrist
or when I made a woman who was really beautiful
love me when she didn't want to
it must be the warm weather
I think
I could smash bricks with my bare hands
or screw
until I was half out of my mind

the only trouble
jesus the only trouble
is I keep thinking about a kid I saw starving on television
last night from Biafra he was unbearably fragile
his stomach puffed up arms and legs sticks eyes distorted
what if I touched somebody like that when I was this way?
I can feel him going stiff under my hands
I can feel his belly bulging ready to pop
his pale hair disengaging from its roots like something awful and alive
please

I won't hurt you I want you in my arms
I want to make something for you to eat like warm soup
look I'll chew the meat for you first
in case your teeth ache
I'll keep everybody away if you're sleeping
and hold you next to me like a little brother when we go out
I'm so cold now
what are we going to do with all this?
I promise I won't feel myself like this ever again
it's just the spring it doesn't mean anything please

Yours

I'd like every girl in the world to have a poem of her own
I've written for her I don't even want to make love to them all anymore
just write things your body makes me delirious your face enchants me
you are a wonder of soul spirit intelligence one for every one
and then the men I don't care whether I can still beat them all
them too a poem for them how many?
seeing you go through woods like part of the woods seeing you play piano
seeing you hold your child in your tender devastating hands
and of course the children too little poems they could sing or dance to
this is our jumping game this our seeing game our holding each other
even the presidents with all their death the congressmen and judges
I'd give them something
they would hold awed to their chests as their proudest life thing
somebody walking along a road where there's no city would look up
and see his poem coming down like a feather out of nowhere
or on the assembly line new instructions a voice sweet as lunchtime
or she would turn over a stone by the fire and if she couldn't read
it would sing to her in her body
listen! everyone! you have your own poem now
it's yours as much as your heart as much as your own life is
you can do things to it shine it iron it dress it in doll clothes
o men! o people! please stop how it's happening now please
I'm working as fast as I can I can't stop to use periods
sometimes I draw straight lines on the page because the words
are too slow
I can only do one at a time don't die first please
don't give up and start crying or hating each other they're coming
I'm hurrying be patient there's still time isn't there? isn't there?

The Nickname of Hell

the president of my country his face flushed
horribly like a penis is walking through
the schoolyard toward my daughter I tell him
mr president I will make it all right but
under his hand his penis is lined with many
buttons I tell him the orders are changing
but commanders deep in his penis prime it
I tell him about love I tell him there
is a new god who believes anything I
cringe alongside him I dance like a daughter
it is the schoolyard the daughters play
on the dangerous fences I tell him I love
him I tell him the daughters aren't here
even he is holding me now his arms hold
me his lips you are my bliss he tells me
these are my arms these my lips you
are my penis he tells me his face stings
into mine like a penis you are my joy you
my daughter hold me my daughter my daughter

The Rampage

a baby got here once who before
he was all the way out and could already feel the hindu
pain inside him and the hebrew and the iliad
decided he was never going to stop crying no matter what
until they did something he wasn't going
to turn the horror
off in their fat sentences
and in the light bulb how much murder to get light
and in the walls agony agony for the bricks for the glaze
he was going to keep screaming
until they made death little like he was
and loved him too and sent
him back to undo all this
and it happened
he kept screaming he scared them he saw them
filling with womblight again like stadiums
he saw the tears sucked back into the story the smiles
opening like sandwiches
so he stopped
and looked up and said all right
it's better now
I'm hungry now I want just to sleep
and they let him

FROM

The Lark. The Thrush.

The Starling.

(POEMS FROM ISSA)

[1 9 8 3]

In the next life,
butterfly,
a thousand years from now,

we'll sit like this
again
under the tree

in the dust,
hearing it, this
great thing.

I sit in my room.

Outside, haze.

The whole world
is haze

and I can't figure out
one room.

That the world
is going
to end someday
does not concern
the wren:

it's time to
build your nest,
you build
your nest.

Listen carefully.

I'm meditating.
The only thing in my mind
right now
is the wind.

No, wait . . . the autumn
wind, that's right,
the *autumn* wind!

What we are
given:
resignation.

What is
taken from us:
resignation.

It is ours that
we can see, do
see, must see

our own bones
bleaching
under the warm moon.

In the middle
of a bite of
grass,
the turtle stops
to listen for,
oh, an
hour, two
hours,
three hours . . .

This is what,
at last, it is
to be
a human being.

Leaving nothing
out, not
one star, one
wren, one tear
out.

That night,
winter,
rain,
the mountains.

No guilt. No
not-guilt.
Winter,
rain,
mountains.

I know
nothing anymore
of roads.

Winter
is a road,
I know,

but the body,
the beloved
body,

is it, too,
only a kind
of road?

Did I write this
as I was
dying?

Did I really
write
this?

That I wanted to thank
the snow
fallen on my blanket?

Could I
have written
this?

41

FROM

With Ignorance

[1 9 7 7]

The Sanctity

for Nick and Arlene de Credico

The men working on the building going up here have got these great,
little motorized wheelbarrows that're supposed to be for lugging bricks
    and mortar
but that they seem to spend most of their time barrel-assing up the street
    in,
racing each other or trying to con the local secretaries into taking rides
    in the bucket.
I used to work on jobs like that and now when I pass by the skeleton of
    the girders
and the tangled heaps of translucent brick wrappings, I remember the
    guys I was with then
and how hard they were to know. Some of them would be so good to
    be with at work,
slamming things around, playing practical jokes, laughing all the time,
    but they could be miserable,
touchy and sullen, always ready to imagine an insult or get into a fight
    anywhere else.
If something went wrong, if a compressor blew or a truck backed over
    somebody,
they'd be the first ones to risk their lives dragging you out
but later you'd see them and they'd be drunk, looking for trouble, almost
    murderous,
and it would be frightening trying to figure out which person they really
    were.
Once I went home to dinner with a carpenter who'd taken me under his
    wing
and was keeping everyone off my back while he helped me. He was
    beautiful but at his house, he sulked.
After dinner, he and the kids and I were watching television while his
    wife washed the dishes
and his mother, who lived with them, sat at the table holding a big
    cantaloupe in her lap,
fondling it and staring at it with the kind of intensity people usually only
    look into fires with.

The wife kept trying to take it away from her but the old lady squawked
and my friend said, "Leave her alone, will you?" "But she's doing it on
purpose," the wife said.
I was watching. The mother put both her hands on it then, with her
thumbs spread,
as though the melon were a head and her thumbs were covering the eyes
and she was aiming it like a gun or a camera.
Suddenly the wife muttered, "You bitch!" ran over to the bookshelf, took
a book down—
A *History of Revolutions*—rattled through the pages and triumphantly
handed it to her husband.
A photograph: someone who's been garroted and the executioner, stand-
ing behind him in a business hat,
has his thumbs just like that over the person's eyes, straightening the
head,
so that you thought the thumbs were going to move away because they
were only pointing
the person at something they wanted him to see and the one with the
hands was going to say, "Look! Right there!"
"I told you," the wife said. "I swear to god she's trying to drive me crazy."
I didn't know what it all meant but my friend went wild, started breaking
things, I went home
and when I saw him the next morning at breakfast he acted as though
nothing had happened.
We used to eat at the Westfield truck stop, but I remember Fritz's, The
Victory, The Eagle,
and I think I've never had as much contentment as I did then, before
work, the light just up,
everyone sipping their coffee out of the heavy white cups and teasing the
middle-aged waitresses
who always acted vaguely in love with whoever was on jobs around there
right then
besides the regular farmers on their way back from the markets and the
long-haul truckers.
Listen: sometimes when you go to speak about life it's as though your
mouth's full of nails
but other times it's so easy that it's ridiculous to even bother.

The eggs and the toast could fly out of the plates and it wouldn't matter
and the bubbles in the level could blow sky-high and it still wouldn't.
Listen to the back-hoes gearing up and the shouts and somebody cracking
        his sledge into the mortar pan.
Listen again. He'll do it all day if you want him to. Listen again.

Spit

*. . . then the son of the "superior race" began to spit into the Rabbi's mouth so that the
Rabbi could continue to spit on the Torah . . .*

—THE BLACK BOOK

After this much time, it's still impossible. The SS man with his stiff hair
    and his uniform;
the Rabbi, probably in a torn overcoat, probably with a stained beard the
    other would be clutching;
the Torah, God's word, on the altar, the letters blurring under the blended
    phlegm;
the Rabbi's parched mouth, the SS man perfectly absorbed, obsessed with
    perfect humiliation.
So many years and what is there to say still about the soldiers waiting
    impatiently in the snow,
about the one stamping his feet, thinking, Kill him! Get it over with!
while back there the lips of the Rabbi and the other would have brushed
and if time had stopped you would have thought they were lovers,
so lightly kissing, the sharp, luger hand under the dear chin,
the eyes furled slightly and then when it started again the eyelashes of
    both of them
shyly fluttering as wonderfully as the pulse of a baby.
Maybe we don't have to speak of it at all, it's still the same.
War, that happens and stops happening but is always somehow right
    there, twisting and hardening us;
then what we make of God—words, spit, degradation, murder, shame;
    every conceivable torment.
All these ways to live that have something to do with how we live
and that we're almost ashamed to use as metaphors for what goes on in
    us
but that we do anyway, so that love is battle and we watch ourselves in
    love
become maddened with pride and incompletion, and God is what it is
    when we're alone
wrestling with solitude and everything speaking in our souls turns against
    us like His fury

and just facing another person, there is so much terror and hatred that
    yes,
spitting in someone's mouth, trying to make him defile his own meaning,
would signify the struggle to survive each other and what we'll enact to
    accomplish it.

There's another legend.
It's about Moses, that when they first brought him as a child before
    Pharaoh,
the king tested him by putting a diamond and a live coal in front of him
and Moses picked up the red ember and popped it into his mouth
so for the rest of his life he was tongue-tied and Aaron had to speak for
    him.
What must his scarred tongue have felt like in his mouth?
It must have been like always carrying something there that weighed too
    much,
something leathery and dead whose greatest gravity was to loll out like
    an ox's,
and when it moved, it must have been like a thick embryo slowly coming
    alive,
butting itself against the inner sides of his teeth and cheeks.
And when God burned in the bush, how could he not cleave to him?
How could he not know that all of us were on fire and that every word
    we said would burn forever,
in pain, unquenchably, and that God knew it, too, and would say nothing
    Himself ever again beyond this,
ever, but would only live in the flesh that we use like firewood,
in all the caves of the body, the gut cave, the speech cave:
He would slobber and howl like something just barely a man that beats
    itself again and again onto the dark,
moist walls away from the light, away from whatever would be light for
    this last eternity.
"Now therefore go," He said, "and I will be with thy mouth."

Toil

After the argument—argument? battle, war, harrowing; you need shrieks,
    moans from the pit—
after that woman and I anyway stop raking each other with the meat-
    hooks we've become with each other,
I fit my forehead into the smudge I've already sweated onto the window
    with a thousand other exhaustions
and watch an old man having breakfast out of a pile of bags on my front
    step.
Peas from a can, bread with the day-old price scrawled over the label in
    big letters
and then a bottle that looks so delectable, the way he carefully unsheathes
    it
so the neck just lips out of the wrinkled foreskin of the paper and closes
    his eyes and tilts,
long and hard, that if there were one lie left in me to forgive a last rapture
    of cowardice
I'd go down there too and sprawl and let the whole miserable rest go to
    pieces.
Does anyone still want to hear how love can turn rotten?
How you can be so desperate that even going adrift wouldn't be
    enough—
you want to scour yourself out, get rid of all the needs you've still got in
    yourself
that keep you endlessly tearing against yourself in rages of guilt and
    frustration?
I don't. I'd rather think about other things. Beauty. How do you learn
    to believe there's beauty?
The kids going by on their way to school with their fat little lunch bags:
    beauty!
My old drunk with his bags—bottle bags, rag bags, shoe bags: beauty!
    beauty!
He lies there like the goddess of wombs and first-fruit, asleep in the
    riches,
one hand still hooked in mid-flight over the intricacies of the iron railing.

50

Old father, wouldn't it be a good ending if you and I could just walk
    away together?
Or that you were the king who reveals himself, who folds back the barbed,
    secret wings
and we're all so in love now, one spirit, one flesh, one generation, that
    the truces don't matter?
Or maybe a better ending would be that there is no ending.
Maybe the Master of Endings is wandering down through his herds to
    find it
and the cave cow who tells truth and the death cow who holds sea in
    her eyes are still there
but all he hears are the same old irresistible slaughter-pen bawlings.
So maybe there is no end to the story and maybe there's no story.
Maybe the last calf just ambles up to the trough through the clearing
and nudges aside the things that swarm on the water and her mouth dips
    in among them and drinks.
Then she lifts, and it pours, everything, gushes, and we're lost in both
    waters.

The Last Deaths

1

A few nights ago I was half-watching the news on television and half-
reading to my daughter.
The book was about a boy who makes a zoo out of junk he finds in a
lot—
I forget exactly; a horse-bottle, a bedspring that's a snake, things like
that—
and on the news they were showing a film about the most recent bomb-
ings.
There was a woman crying, tearing at her hair and breasts, shrieking
incomprehensibly
because her husband and all her children had been killed the night before
and just when she'd flung herself against the legs of one of the soldiers
watching her,
Jessie looked up and said, "What's the matter with her? Why's she crying?"

2

I haven't lived with my daughter for a year now and sometimes it still
hurts not to be with her more,
not to have her laughter when I want it or to be able to comfort her
when she cries out in her sleep.
I don't see her often enough to be able to know what I can say to her,
what I can solve for her without introducing more confusions than there
were in the first place.
That's what happened with death. She was going to step on a bug and
when I told her she'd kill it,
it turned out that no one had ever told her about death and now she had
to know.
"It's when you don't do anything anymore," I told her. "It's like being
asleep."
I didn't say for how long but she's still been obsessed with it since then,

wanting to know if she's going to die and when and if I am and her
        mother and grandma and do robbers do it?
Maybe I should have just given her the truth, but I didn't: now what was
        I going to say about that woman?
"Her house fell down," I said. "Who knocked down her house?" "It just
        fell."
Then I found something for us to do, but last night, again, first thing,
"Tell me about that girl." "What girl?" "You know." Of course I know.
What could have gone on in my child's dreams last night so that woman
        was a girl now?
How many times must they have traded places back and forth in that
        innocent crib?
"You mean the lady whose house fell down?" "Yeah, who knocked her
        house down?"

3

These times. The endless wars. The hatreds. The vengefulness.
Everyone I know getting out of their marriage. Old friends distrustful.
The politicians using us until you can't think about it anymore because
        you can't tell anymore
which reality affects which and how do you escape from it without
        everything battering you back again?
How many times will I lie to Jessie about things that have no meaning
        for either of us?
How many forgivenesses will I need from her when all I wanted was to
        keep her from suffering the same ridiculous illusions I have?
There'll be peace soon.
They'll fling it down like sick meat we're supposed to lick up and be
        thankful for and what then?

4

Jessie, it's as though the whole race is sunk in an atmosphere of blood
and it's been clotting for so many centuries we can hardly move now.
Someday, you and I will face each other and turn away and the absence,
the dread, will flame between us like an enormous, palpable word that
        wasn't spoken.

Do we only love because we're weak and murderous?
Are we commended to each other to alleviate our terror of solitude and
    annihilation and that's all?

5

I wish I could change dreams with you, baby. I've had the bad ones,
    what comes now is calm and abstract.
Last night, while you and that poor woman were trading deaths like
    horrible toys,
I was dreaming about the universe. The whole universe was happening
    in one day, like a blossom,
and during that day people's voices kept going out to it, crying, "Stop!
    Stop!"
The universe didn't mind, though. It knew we were only cursing love
    again
because we didn't know how to love, not even for a day,
but our little love days were just seeds it blew out on parachutes into the
    summer wind.
Then you and I were there. We shouted "Stop!" too. We kept wanting
    the universe to explode,
we kept wishing it would go back into its root, but the universe understood.
We were its children. It let us cry into its petals, it let its stems bend
    against us,
then it fed and covered us and we looked up sleepily—it was time to
    sleep—
and whatever our lives were, our love, this once, was enough.

Bob

If you put in enough hours in bars, sooner or later you get to hear every
    imaginable kind of bullshit.
Every long-time loser has a history to convince you he isn't living at the
    end of his own leash
and every kid has some pimple on his psyche he's trying to compensate
    for with an epic,
but the person with the most unlikely line I'd ever heard—he told me
    he'd killed, more than a few times,
during the war and then afterwards working for the mob in Phila-
    delphia—I could never make up my mind about.
He was big, bigger than big. He'd also been drinking hard and wanted
    to be everyone's friend
and until the bartender called the cops because he wouldn't stop stuffing
    money in girls' blouses,
he gave me his life: the farm childhood, the army, re-upping, the war
    —that killing—
coming back and the new job—that killing—then almost being killed
    himself by another hood and a kind of pension,
a distributorship, incredibly enough, for hairdresser supplies in the ward
    around Passyunk and Mifflin.
He left before the cops came, and before he left he shook my hand and
    looked into my eyes.
It's impossible to tell how much that glance weighed: it was like having
    to lift something,
something so ponderous and unwieldy that you wanted to call for someone
    to help you
and when he finally turned away, it wouldn't have bothered me at all if
    I'd never seen him again.

This is going to get a little nutty now, maybe because everything was a
    little nutty for me back then.
Not a little. I'd been doing some nice refining. No work, no woman,
    hardly any friends left.

The details don't matter. I was helpless, self-pitying, angry, inert, and
        right now
I was flying to Detroit to interview for a job I knew I wouldn't get. Outside,
the clouds were packed against our windows and just as I let my book
        drop to look out,
we broke through into a sky so brilliant that I had to close my eyes against
        the glare.
I stayed like that, waiting for the stinging after-light to fade, but it seemed
        to pulse instead,
then suddenly it washed strangely through me, swelling, powdering,
and when my sight came back, I was facing inwards, into the very center
        of myself,
a dark, craggy place, and there was a sound that when I blocked the jets,
the hiss of the pressurization valves and the rattling silverware and glasses,
        I realized was laughter.
The way I was then, I think nothing could have shocked me. I was a
        well, I'd fallen in,
someone was there with me, but all I did was drift until I came to him:
        a figure, arms lifted,
he was moving in a great, cumbersome dance, full of patience, full of
        time, and that laughter,
a deep, flowing tumult of what seemed to be songs from someone else's
        life.
Now the strange part. My ears were ringing, my body felt like water, but
        I moved again,
farther in, until I saw the face of who it was with me and it was Bob,
        the drunk,
or if it wasn't him, his image filled the space, the blank, the template,
        better than anyone else,
and so, however doubtful it seems now, I let it be him: he was there, I
        let him stay.
Understand, this happened quickly. By that night, home again, I was
        broken again,
torn, crushed on the empty halves of my bed, but for that time, from
        Pittsburgh, say,
until we braked down to the terminal in Detroit, I smiled at that self in
        myself,

his heavy dance, his laughter winding through the wrack and detritus of
    what I thought I was.

Bob, I don't know what happened to. He probably still makes the circuits
    of the clubs and corner bars,
and there must be times when strangers listen and he can tell it, the truth
    or his nightmare of it.
"I killed people," the secret heart opening again, "and Jesus God, I didn't
    even know them."

Bread

A whole section of the city I live in has been urban renewed, some of it
    torn down,
some restored to what it was supposed to have been a few hundred years
    ago.
Once you could've walked blocks without hearing English, now the
    ghettos have been cleared,
there are parks and walkways and the houses are all owned by people
    who've moved back from the suburbs.
When I lived there, at the very edge of it where the expressway is going
    in now
and the buildings are still boarded with plywood or flattened altogether,
the old market was already shuttered, the shipping depots had been re-
    located upriver
and the only person I ever saw was a grocer who lived across from me
    over his empty store.
I couldn't understand what he was doing there—it must have been years
since a customer had come in past the dead register and the icebox
    propped open with a carton,
but it was comforting to have him: he'd make his bed, sweep, cook for
    himself like a little wife
and when the constables came every week or so to tell us we were
    condemned,
he never paid attention so I didn't either. I didn't want to leave. I'd been
    in love,
I thought I was healing, for all I know I might have stayed forever in the
    grim room I was camped in
but one day some boys who must have climbed up through one of the
    abandoned tenements
suddenly appeared skidding and wrestling over the steep pitch of the old
    man's roof
and when I shouted at them to get the hell off, he must have thought
    I'd meant him:
he lurched in his bed and stopped rubbing himself with the white cream
    he used to use on his breasts.

He looked up, our eyes met, and I think for the first time he really
     believed I was there.
I don't know how long we stared at each other—I could hear the kids
     shrieking at me
and the road-building equipment that had just started tearing the skin
     from the avenue—
then his zincy fingers slowly subsided against his heart and he smiled,
a brilliant, total, incongruous smile, and even though I had no desire
     to,
the way afterwards I had no desire to cry when my children were born,
     but did,
sobbed, broke down with joy or some inadmissible apprehension, I smiled
     back.
It was as though we were lovers, as though, like lovers, we'd made speech
     again
and were listening as it gutted and fixed the space between us and then
     a violent,
almost physical loathing took me, for all I'd done to have ended in this
     place,
to myself, to everyone, to the whole business we're given the name life
     for.

I could go on with this. I could call it a victory, an exemplary triumph,
     but I'd lie.
Sometimes the universe inside us can assume the aspect of places we've
     been
so that instead of emotions we see trees we knew or touched or a path,
and instead of the face of a thought, there'll be an unmade bed, a car
     nosing from an alley.
All I know about that time is that it stayed, that something, pain or the
     fear of it,
makes me stop the wheel and reach to the silence beyond my eyes and
     it's still there:
the empty wind, the white crosses of the renewers slashed on the
     doorposts,
the last, dim layers of paint loosening from the rotted sills, drifting
     downwards.

Near the Haunted Castle

Teen Gangs Fight: Girl Paralyzed by Police Bullet

—HEADLINE

This is a story. You don't have to think about it, it's make-believe.
It's like a lie, maybe not quite a lie but I don't want you to worry about
      it.
The reason it's got to be a lie is because you already know the truth and
      I already know it
and what difference does it make? We still can't do anything: why kill
      yourself?
So here's the story. It's like the princess and the pea, remember?
Where they test her with mattresses and a pea and she's supposed not to
      sleep
and get upset and then they'll know she's the princess and marry her?
Except in this version, she comes in and nobody believes it's her and
      they lay her down
but instead of forty mattresses do you know what they lay her on? Money!
Of course, money! A million dollars! It's like a hundred mattresses, it's
      so soft, a thousand!
It's how much you cut from the budget for teachers to give the policemen.
It's how much you take from relief to trade for bullets. Soft!
And instead of the pea, what? A bullet! Brilliant! A tiny bullet stuck in
      at the bottom!
So then comes the prince. My prince, my beauty. Except he has holsters.
He has leather and badges. And what he does, he starts tearing the
      mattresses out.
Out? Don't forget, it's a story. Don't forget to not worry, it's pretend.
He's tearing the mattresses out and then he's stuffing them in his mouth!
This wonderful prince-mouth, this story-mouth, it holds millions,
      billions,
and she's falling, slowly, or no, the pea, the bullet, is rising,
surging like some ridiculous funny snout out of the dark down there.
Does it touch you? Oh, yes, but don't worry, this is just a fib, right?
It slides next to your skin and it's cold and it goes in, in! as though you
      were a door,

as though you were the whole bedroom; in, through the backbone,
    through the cartilage,
the cords, then it freezes. It freezes and the prince is all gone,
this is the sleeping, the wrong-sleeping, you shouldn't be sleeping,
the so-heaviness in the arms, the so-heaviness in the legs, don't sleep,
    they'll leave you,
they'll throw you away . . . the dollars spinning, the prince leaving,
and you, at the bottom, on the no-turning, on the pea, like a story,
on the bullet, the single bullet that costs next to nothing, like one dollar.
People torture each other so they'll tell the whole truth, right?
And study the nervous systems of the lower orders to find the truth, right?
And tell the most obviously absurd tales for the one grain of truth?
The mother puts down her book and falls asleep watching television.
On the television they go on talking.
The father's in bed, the little gears still rip through his muscles.
The two brothers have the same dream, like Blinken and Nod, like the
    mayor and the president.
The sister . . . The sister . . . The heart furnace, the brain furnace, hot
    . . . hot . . .
Let's go back to find where the truth is. Let's find the beginning.
In the beginning was love, right? No, in the beginning . . . the
    bullet . . .

The Cave

I think most people are relieved the first time they actually know someone
who goes crazy.
It doesn't happen the way you hear about it where the person gibbers
and sticks to you like an insect:
mostly there's crying, a lot of silence, sometimes someone will whisper
back to their voices.
All my friend did was sit, at home until they found him, then for hours
at a time on his bed in the ward,
pointing at his eyes, chanting the same phrase over and over. "Too much
fire!" he'd say. "Too much fire!"
I remember I was amazed at how raggedy he looked, then annoyed
because he wouldn't answer me
and then, when he was getting better, I used to pester him to tell me
about that fire-thing.
He'd seemed to be saying he'd seen too much and I wanted to know too
much what
because my obsession then was that I was somehow missing everything
beyond the ordinary.
What was only real was wrong. There were secrets that could turn you
into stone,
they were out of range or being kept from me, but my friend, if he knew
what I meant, wouldn't say,
so we'd talk politics or books or moon over a beautiful girl who was
usually in the visiting room when we were
who mutilated herself. Every time I was there, new slashes would've
opened out over her forearms and wrists
and once there were two brilliant medallions on her cheeks that I thought
were rouge spots
but that my friend told me were scratches she'd put there with a broken
light bulb when she'd run away the day before.
The way you say running away in hospitals is "eloping." Someone who
hurts themself is a "cutter."
How could she do it to herself? My friend didn't think that was the
question.

She'd eloped, cut, they'd brought her back and now she was waiting
    there again,
those clowny stigmata of lord knows what on her, as tranquil and seductive
    as ever.
I used to storm when I'd leave her there with him. She looked so
    vulnerable.
All the hours they'd have. I tormented myself imagining how they'd come
    together,
how they'd tell each other the truths I thought I had to understand to
    live,
then how they'd kiss, their lips, chaste and reverent, rushing over the
    forgiven surfaces.
Tonight, how long afterwards, watching my wife undress, letting my gaze
    go so everything blurs
but the smudges of her nipples and hair and the wonderful lumpy graces
    of her pregnancy,
I still can bring it back: those dismal corridors, the furtive nods, the
    moans I thought were sexual
and the awful lapses that seemed vestiges of exaltations I would never
    have,
but now I know whatever in the mystery I was looking for, whatever brute
    or cloud I thought eluded me,
isn't lost in the frenzy of one soul or another, but next to us, in the
    touch, between.
Lying down, fumbling for the light, moving into the shadow with my
    son or daughter, I find it again:
the prism of hidden sorrow, the namelessness of nothing and nothing
    shuddering across me,
and then the warmth, clinging and brightening, the hide, the caul, the
    first mind.

Hog Heaven

for James Havard

It stinks. It stinks and it stinks and it stinks and it stinks.
It stinks in the mansions and it stinks in the shacks and the carpeted
      offices,
in the beds and the classrooms and out in the fields where there's no
      one.
It just stinks. Sniff and feel it come up: it's like death coming up.
Take one foot, ignore it long enough, leave it on the ground long enough
because you're afraid to stop, even to love, even to be loved,
it'll stink worse than you can imagine, as though the whole air was meat
      pressing your eyelids,
as though you'd been caught, hung up from the earth
and all the stinks of the fear drain down and your toes are the valves
      dripping
the giant stinks of the pain and the death and the radiance.
Old people stink, with their teeth and their hot rooms, and the kiss,
the age-kiss, the death-kiss, it comes like a wave and you want to fall
      down and be over.
And money stinks: the little threads that go through it like veins through
      an eye,
each stinks—if you hold it onto your lip it goes bad, it stinks like a vein
      going bad.
And Christ stank: he knew how the slaves would be stacked into the holds
      and he took it—
the stink of the vomit and shit and of somebody just rolling over and
      plunging in with his miserable seed.
And the seed stinks. And the fish carrying it upstream and the bird eating
      the fish
and you the bird's egg, the dribbles of yolk, the cycle: the whole thing
      stinks.
The intellect stinks and the moral faculty, like things burning, like the
      cave under justice,
and the good quiet men, like oceans of tears squeezed into one handful,
      they stink,

and the whole consciousness, like something plugged up, stinks, like
    something cut off.
Life stinks and death stinks and god and your hand touching your face
and every breath, daring to turn, daring to come back from the stop: the
    turn stinks
and the last breath, the real one, the one where everyone troops into
    your bed
and piles on—oh, that one stinks best! It stays on your mouth
and who you kiss now knows life and knows death, knows how it would
    be to fume in a nostril
and the thousand desires that stink like the stars and the voice heard
    through the stars
and each time—milk sour, egg sour, sperm sour—each time—dirt,
    friend, father—
each time—mother, tree, breath—each time—breath and breath and
    breath—
each time the same stink, the amazement, the wonder to do this and it
    flares,
this, and it stinks, this: it stinks and it stinks and it stinks and it stinks.

Blades

When I was about eight, I once stabbed somebody, another kid, a little girl.

I'd been hanging around in front of the supermarket near our house

and when she walked by, I let her have it, right in the gap between her shirt and her shorts

with a piece of broken-off car antenna I used to carry around in my pocket.

It happened so fast I still don't know how I did it: I was as shocked as she was

except she squealed and started yelling as though I'd plunged a knife in her

and everybody in the neighborhood gathered around us, then they called the cops,

then the girl's mother came running out of the store saying, "What happened? What happened?"

and the girl screamed, "He stabbed me!" and I screamed back, "I did not!" and she you did too

and me I didn't and we were both crying hysterically by that time.

Somebody pulled her shirt up and it was just a scratch but we went on and on

and the mother, standing between us, seemed to be absolutely terrified.

I still remember how she watched first one of us and then the other with a look of complete horror—

You did too! I did not!—as though we were both strangers, as though it was some natural disaster

she was beholding that was beyond any mode of comprehension so all she could do

was stare speechlessly at us, and then another expression came over her face,

one that I'd never seen before, that made me think she was going to cry herself

and sweep both of us, the girl and me, into her arms to hold us against her.

The police came just then, though, quieted everyone down, put the girl
     and the mother
into a squad car to take to the hospital and me in another to take to jail
except they really only took me around the corner and let me go because
     the mother and daughter were black
and in those days you had to do something pretty terrible to get into
     trouble that way.

I don't understand how we twist these things or how we get them straight
     again
but I relived that day I don't know how many times before I realized I
     had it all wrong.
The boy wasn't me at all, he was another kid: I was just there.
And it wasn't the girl who was black, but him. The mother was real,
     though.
I really had thought she was going to embrace them both
and I had dreams about her for years afterwards: that I'd be being born
     again
and she'd be lifting me with that same wounded sorrow or she would
     suddenly appear out of nowhere,
blotting out everything but a single, blazing wing of holiness.
Who knows the rest? I can still remember how it felt the old way.
How I make my little thrust, how she crushes us against her, how I turn
     and snarl
at the cold circle of faces around us because something's torn in me,
some ancient cloak of terror we keep on ourselves because we'll do
     anything,
anything, not to know how silently we knell in the mouth of death
and not to obliterate the forgiveness and the lies we offer one another
     and call innocence.
This is innocence. I touch her, we kiss.
And this. I'm here or not here. I can't tell. I stab her. I stab her again.
     I still can't.

The Shade

A summer cold. No rash. No fever. Nothing. But a dozen times during
   the night I wake
to listen to my son whimpering in his sleep, trying to snort the sticky
   phlegm out of his nostrils.
The passage clears, silence, nothing. I cross the room, groping for the
   warm,
elusive creature of his breath and my heart lunges, stutters, tries to race
   away;
I don't know from what, from my imagination, from life itself, maybe
   from understanding too well
and being unable to do anything about how much of my anxiety is always
   for myself.
Whatever it was, I left it when the dawn came. There's a park near here
where everyone who's out of work in our neighborhood comes to line
   up in the morning.
The converted school buses shuttling hands to the cannery fields in Jersey
   were just rattling away when I got there
and the small-time contractors, hiring out cheap walls, cheap ditches,
   cheap everything,
were loading laborers onto the sacks of plaster and concrete in the backs
   of their pickups.
A few housewives drove by looking for someone to babysit or clean cellars
   for them,
then the gates of the local bar unlaced and whoever was left drifted in
   out of the wall of heat
already rolling in with the first fists of smoke from the city incinerators.

It's so quiet now, I can hear the sparrows foraging scraps of garbage on
   the paths.
The stove husk chained as a sign to the store across the street creaks in
   the last breeze of darkness.
By noon, you'd have to be out of your mind to want to be here: the park
   will reek of urine,

bodies will be sprawled on the benches, men will wrestle through the
surf of broken bottles,
but even now, watching the leaves of the elms softly lifting toward the
day, softly falling back,
all I see is fear forgiving fear on every page I turn; all I know is every
time I try to change it,
I say it again: my wife, my child . . . my home, my work, my sorrow.
If this were the last morning of the world, if time had finally moved
inside us and erupted
and we were Agamemnon again, Helen again, back on that faint, be-
ginning planet
where even the daily survivals were giants, filled with light, I think I'd
still be here,
afraid or not enough afraid, silently howling the names of death over the
grass and asphalt.
The morning goes on, the sun burning, the earth burning, and between
them, part of me lifts and starts back,
past the wash of dead music from the bar, the drinker reeling on the
curb, the cars coughing alive,
and part, buried in itself, stays, forever, blinking into the glare, freezing.

With Ignorance

With ignorance begins a knowledge the first characteristic of which is ignorance.
— K I E R K E G A A R D

1

Again and again. Again lips, again breast, again hand, thigh, loin and
    bed and bed
after bed, the hunger, hunger again, need again, the rising, the spasm
    and needing again.
Flesh, lie, confusion and loathing, the scabs of clear gore, the spent seed
    and the spurt
of desire that seemed to generate from itself, from its own rising and
    spasm.
Everything waste, everything would be or was, the touching, the touch
    and the touch back.
Everything rind, scar, without sap, without meaning or seed, and every-
    one, everyone else,
every slip or leap into rage, every war, flame, sob, it was there, too, the
    stifling, the hushed,
malevolent frenzy and croak of desire, again and again, the same hunger,
    same need.
Touch me, hold me, sorrow and sorrow, the emptied, emptied again,
    touched again.
The hunger, the rising, again and again until again itself seemed to be
    need and hunger
and so much terror could rise out of that, the hunger repeating itself out
    of the fear now,
that how could you know if you lived within it at all, if there wasn't
    another,
a malediction or old prayer, a dream or a city of dream or a single,
    fleshless, dreamless error,
whose tongue you were, who spoke with you, butted or rasped with you,
    but still, tongue or another,
word or not word, what could it promise that wouldn't drive us back to
    the same hunger and sorrow?

What could it say that wouldn't spasm us back to ourselves to be bait or
a dead prayer?
Or was that it? Only that? The prayer hunting its prey, hunting the bait
of itself?
Was the hunger the faith in itself, the belief in itself, even the prayer?
Was it the dead prayer?

2

The faces waver; each gathers the others within it, the others shuddering
through it
as though there were tides or depths, as though the depths, the tides of
the eyes themselves
could throw out refractions, waves, shifts and wavers and each faceless
refraction
could rise to waver beneath me, to shift, to be faceless again, beneath
or within me,
the lying, confusion, recurrence, reluctance, the surge through into
again.
Each room, each breast finding its ripeness of shadow, each lip and its
shadow,
the dimming, flowing, the waver through time, through loss, gone,
irredeemable,
all of it, each face into regret, each room into forgetting and absence.
But still, if there were a moment, still, one moment, to begin in or go
back to,
to return to move through, waver through, only a single moment carved
back from the lie
the way the breast is carved from its shadow, sealed from the dross of
darkness
until it takes the darkness itself and fills with it, taking the breath;
if, in the return, I could be taken the way I could have been taken, with
voice or breast,
emptied against the space of the breast as though breast was breath and
my breath,
taken, would have been emptied into the moment, it could rise here,
now, in that moment, the same moment.

But it won't, doesn't. The moments lift and fall, break, and it shifts,
   wavers,
subsides into the need again, the faceless again, the faceless and the lie.

3

Remorse? Blame? There is a pit-creature. The father follows it down with
   the ax.
Exile and sorrow. Once there were things we lived in, don't you re-
   member?
We scraped, starved, then we came up, abashed, to the sun, and what
   was the first word?
Blame, blame and remorse, then sorrow, then the blame was the father
   then was ourselves.
Such a trite story, do we have to retell it? The mother took back the sun
   and we . . .
Remorse, self-regard, call it shame or being abashed or trying again, for
   the last time, to return.
Remorse, then power, the power and the blame and what did we ever
   suffer but power?
The head lifting itself, then the wars, remorse and revenge, the wars of
   humility,
the blades and the still valley, the double intention, the simple tree in
   the blood.
Then exile again, even the sword, even the spear, the formula scratched
   on the sand,
even the christening, the christened, blame again, power again, but even
   then,
taken out of the fire at the core and never returned, what could we not
   sanction?
One leg after the other, the look back, the power, the fire again and the
   sword again.
Blame and remorse. That gives into desire again, into hunger again. That
   gives into . . . this . . .

4

Someone . . . Your arm touches hers or hers finds yours, unmoving,
    unasking.
A silence, as though for the first time, and as though for the first time,
    you can listen,
as though there were chords: your life, then the other's, someone else,
    as though for the first time.
The life of the leaves over the streetlamp and the glow, swelling, chording,
    under the shadows,
and the quaver of things built, one quavering cell at a time, and the song
of the cell gently bedding itself in its mortar, in this silence, this first
    attempting.
Even the shush of cars, the complex stress of a step, the word called into
    the darkness,
and, wait, the things even beyond, beyond membrane or awareness,
    mode, sense, dream,
don't they sing, too? Chord, too? Isn't the song and the silence there,
    too?
I heard it once. It changed nothing, but once, before I went on, I did
    hear:
the equation of star and planet, the wheel, the ecstasy and division, the
    equation again.
The absolute walking its planks, its long wall, its long chord of laughter
    or grief.
I heard silence, then the children, the spawn, how we have to teach
    every cell how to speak,
and from that, after that, the kiss back from the speech, the touch back
    from the song.
And then more, I heard how it alters, how we, the speakers, the can't-
    live, the refuse-to,
how we, only in darkness, groaning and thrashing into the undergrowth
    of our eternal,
would speak then, would howl, howl again, and at last, at the end, we'd
    hear it:
the prayer and the flesh crying *Why aren't you here?* And the cry back
    in it, *I am! I am!*

5

Imagine dread. Imagine, without symbol, without figure, history or his-
    tories; a place, not a place.
Imagine it must be risen through, beginning with the silent moment,
    the secrets quieted,
one hour, one age at a time, sadness, nostalgia, the absurd pain of
    betrayal.
Through genuine grief, then, through the genuine suffering for the
    boundaries of self
and the touch on the edge, the compassion, that never, never quite,
    breaks through.
Imagine the touch again and beyond it, beyond either end, joy or terror,
    either ending,
the context that gives way, not to death, but past, past anything still with
    a name,
even death, because even death is a promise offering comfort, solace,
    that any direction we turn,
there'll still be the word, the name, and this the promise now, even with
    terror,
the promise again that the wordlessness and the self won't be for one
    instant the same enacting,
and we stay within it, a refusal now, a turning away, a never giving way,
we stay until even extinction itself, the absence, death itself, even death,
    isn't longed for,
never that, but turned toward in the deepest turn of the self, the deepest
    gesture toward self.
And then back, from the dread, from locution and turn, from whatever
    history reflects us,
the self grounds itself again in itself and reflects itself, even its loss, as its
    own,
and back again, still holding itself back, the certainty and belief tearing
    again,
back from the edge of that one flood of surrender which, given space,
    would, like space itself,
rage beyond any limit, the flesh itself giving way in its terror, and back
    from that,

into love, what we have to call love, the one moment before we move
        onwards again,
toward the end, the life again of the self-willed, self-created, embodied,
        reflected again.
Imagine a space prepared for with hunger, with dread, with power and
        the power
over dread which is dread, and the love, with no space for itself, no
        power for itself,
a moment, a silence, a rising, the terror for that, the space for that.
        Imagine love.

6

Morning. The first morning of now. You, your touch, your song and
        morning, but still,
something, a last fear or last lie or last clench of confusion clings,
holds back, refuses, resists, the way fear itself clings in its web of need
        or dread.
What would release be? Being forgiven? No, never forgiven, never only
        forgiven.
To be touched, somehow, with presence, so that the only sign is a step,
        towards or away?
Or not even a step, because the walls, of self, of dread, can never release,
can never forgive stepping away, out of the willed or refused, out of the
        lie or the fear
of the self that still holds back and refuses, resists, and turns back again
        and again into the willed.
What if it could be, though? The first, hectic rush past guilt or remorse?
What if we could find a way through the fires that aren't with us and
        the terrors that are?
What would be there? Would we be thrown back into perhaps or not yet
        or not needed or done?
Could we even slip back, again, past the first step into the first refusal,
the first need, first blot of desire that still somehow exists and wants to
        resist, wants to give back the hard,
immaculate shell of the terror it still keeps against respite and un-
        clenching?

Or perhaps no release, no step or sign, perhaps only to wait and accept.
Perhaps only to bless. To bless and to bless and to bless and to bless.
Willed or unwilled, word or sign, the word suddenly filled with its own
    breath.
Self and other, the self within other and the self still moved through its
    word,
consuming itself, still, and consuming, still being rage, war, the fear,
    the aghast,
but bless, bless still, even the fear, the loss, the gutting of word, the
    gutting even of hunger,
but still to bless and bless, even the turn back, the refusal, to bless and
    to bless and to bless.

7

The first language was loss, the second sorrow, this is the last, then:
    yours . . .
An island, summer, late dusk; hills, laurel and thorn. I walked from the
    harbor, over the cliff road,
down the long trail through the rocks. When I came to our house the
    ship's wake was just edging onto the shore
and on the stone beach, under the cypress, the low waves reassuming
    themselves in the darkness, I waited.
There was a light in a room. You came to it, leaned to it, reaching,
    touching,
and watching you, I saw you give back to the light a light more than
    light
and to the silence you gave more than silence, and, in the silence, I
    heard it.
You, your self, your life, your beginning, pleasure, song clear as the light
    that touched you.
Your will, your given and taken; grief, recklessness, need or desire.
Your passion or tear, step forward or step back into the inevitable veil.
Yours and yours and yours, the dream, the wall of the self that won't be
    or needn't be breached,
and the breach, the touch, yours and the otherness, yours, the sep-
    arateness,

never giving way, never breached really, but as simple, always, as light,
as silence.
This is the language of that, that light and that silence, the silence rising
through or from you.
Nothing to bless or not bless now, nothing to thank or forgive, not to
triumph,
surrender, mean, reveal, assume or exhaust. Our faces bent to the light,
and still,
there is terror, still history, power, grief and remorse, always, always the
self and the other
and the endless tide, the waver, the terror again, between and beneath,
but you, now,
your touch, your light, the otherness yours, the reach, the wheel, the
waves touching.
And to, not wait, not overcome, not even forget or forgive the dream of
the moment, the unattainable moment again.
Your light . . . Your silence . . .
In the silence, without listening, I heard it, and without words, without
language or breath, I answered.

FROM

Tar

[1 9 8 3]

From My Window

Spring: the first morning when that one true block of sweet, laminar,
        complex scent arrives
from somewhere west and I keep coming to lean on the sill, glorying in
        the end of the wretched winter.
The scabby-barked sycamores ringing the empty lot across the way are
        budded—I hadn't noticed—
and the thick spikes of the unlikely urban crocuses have already broken
        the gritty soil.
Up the street, some surveyors with tripods are waving each other left and
        right the way they do.
A girl in a gym suit jogged by a while ago, some kids passed, playing
        hooky, I imagine,
and now the paraplegic Vietnam vet who lives in a half-converted ware-
        house down the block
and the friend who stays with him and seems to help him out come
        weaving towards me,
their battered wheelchair lurching uncertainly from one edge of the side-
        walk to the other.
I know where they're going—to the "Legion": once, when I was putting
        something out, they stopped,
both drunk that time, too, both reeking—it wasn't ten o'clock—and we
        chatted for a bit.
I don't know how they stay alive—on benefits most likely. I wonder if
        they're lovers?
They don't look it. Right now, in fact, they look a wreck, careening
        haphazardly along,
contriving, as they reach beneath me, to dip a wheel from the curb so
        that the chair skewers, teeters,
tips, and they both tumble, the one slowly, almost gracefully sliding in
        stages from his seat,
his expression hardly marking it, the other staggering over him, spinning
        heavily down,
to lie on the asphalt, his mouth working, his feet shoving weakly and
        fruitlessly against the curb.

81

In the storefront office on the corner, Reed and Son, Real Estate, have come to see the show.

Gazing through the golden letters of their name, they're not, at least, thank god, laughing.

Now the buddy, grabbing at a hydrant, gets himself erect and stands there for a moment, panting.

Now he has to lift the other one, who lies utterly still, a forearm shielding his eyes from the sun.

He hauls him partly upright, then hefts him almost all the way into the chair, but a dangling foot

catches a support-plate, jerking everything around so that he has to put him down,

set the chair to rights, and hoist him again and as he does he jerks the grimy jeans right off him.

No drawers, shrunken, blotchy thighs: under the thick, white coils of belly blubber,

the poor, blunt pud, tiny, terrified, retracted, is almost invisible in the sparse genital hair,

then his friend pulls his pants up, he slumps wholly back as though he were, at last, to be let be,

and the friend leans against the cyclone fence, suddenly staring up at me as though he'd known,

all along, that I was watching and I can't help wondering if he knows that in the winter, too,

I watched, the night he went out to the lot and walked, paced rather, almost ran, for how many hours.

It was snowing, the city in that holy silence, the last we have, when the storm takes hold,

and he was making patterns that I thought at first were circles, then realized made a figure eight,

what must have been to him a perfect symmetry but which, from where I was, shivered, bent,

and lay on its side: a warped, unclear infinity, slowly, as the snow came faster, going out.

Over and over again, his head lowered to the task, he slogged the path he'd blazed,

but the race was lost, his prints were filling faster than he made them now and I looked away,

up across the skeletal trees to the tall center city buildings, some, though
    it was midnight,
with all their offices still gleaming, their scarlet warning beacons signaling
    erratically
against the thickening flakes, their smoldering auras softening portions
    of the dim, milky sky.
In the morning, nothing: every trace of him effaced, all the field pure
    white,
its surface glittering, the dawn, glancing from its glaze, oblique, relentless,
    unadorned.

My Mother's Lips

Until I asked her to please stop doing it and was astonished to find that
      she not only could
but from the moment I asked her in fact would stop doing it, my mother,
      all through my childhood,
when I was saying something to her, something important, would move
      her lips as I was speaking
so that she seemed to be saying under her breath the very words I was
      saying as I was saying them.

Or, even more disconcertingly—wildly so now that my puberty had
      erupted—*before* I said them.
When I was smaller, I must just have assumed that she was omniscient.
      Why not?
She knew everything else—when I was tired, or lying; she'd know I was
      ill before I did.
I may even have thought—how could it not have come into my
      mind?—that she *caused* what I said.

All she was really doing of course was mouthing my words a split second
      after I said them myself,
but it wasn't until my own children were learning to talk that I really
      understood how,
and understood, too, the edge of anxiety in it, the wanting to bring you
      along out of the silence,
the compulsion to lift you again from those blank caverns of namelessness
      we encase.

That was long afterward, though: where I was now was just wanting to
      get her to stop,
and, considering how I brooded and raged in those days, how quickly
      my teeth went on edge,
the restraint I approached her with seems remarkable, although her so
      unprotestingly,

readily taming a habit by then three children and a dozen years old was
as much so.

It's endearing to watch us again in that long-ago dusk, facing each other,
my mother and me.
I've just grown to her height, or just past it: there are our lips moving
together,
now the unison suddenly breaks, I have to go on by myself, no maestro,
no score to follow.
I wonder what finally made me take umbrage enough, or heart enough,
to confront her?

It's not important. My cocoon at that age was already unwinding: the
threads ravel and snarl.
When I find one again, it's that two o'clock in the morning, a grim hotel
on a square,
the impenetrable maze of an endless city, when, really alone for the first
time in my life,
I found myself leaning from the window, incanting in a tearing whisper
what I thought were poems.

I'd love to know what I raved that night to the night, what those innocent
dithyrambs were,
or to feel what so ecstatically drew me out of myself and beyond . . .
Nothing is there, though,
only the solemn piazza beneath me, the riot of dim, tiled roofs and
impassable alleys,
my desolate bed behind me, and my voice, hoarse, and the sweet, alien
air against me like a kiss.

The Dog

Except for the dog, that she wouldn't have him put away, wouldn't let
    him die, I'd have liked her.
She was handsome, busty, chunky, early middle-aged, very black, with
    a stiff, exotic dignity
that flurried up in me a mix of warmth and sexual apprehension neither
    of which, to tell the truth,
I tried very hard to nail down: she was that much older and in those days
    there was still the race thing.
This was just at the time of civil rights: the neighborhood I was living in
    was mixed.
In the narrow streets, the tiny three-floored houses they called father-
    son-holy-ghosts
which had been servants' quarters first, workers' tenements, then slums,
    still were, but enclaves of us,
beatniks and young artists, squatted there and commerce between every-
    one was fairly easy.
Her dog, a grinning mongrel, rib and knob, gristle and grizzle, wasn't
    terribly offensive.
The trouble was that he was ill, or the trouble more exactly was that I
    had to know about it.
She used to walk him on a lot I overlooked, he must have had a tumor
    or a blockage of some sort
because every time he moved his bowels, he shrieked, a chilling, almost
    human scream of anguish.
It nearly always caught me unawares, but even when I'd see them first,
    it wasn't better.
The limp leash coiled in her hand, the woman would be profiled to the
    dog, staring into the distance,
apparently oblivious, those breasts of hers like stone, while he, not a step
    away, laboring,
trying to eject the feeble, mucus-coated, blood-flecked chains that finally
    spurted from him,
would set himself on tiptoe and hump into a question mark, one quivering
    back leg grotesquely lifted.

Every other moment he'd turn his head, as though he wanted her, to
      no avail, to look at him,
then his eyes would dim and he'd drive his wounded anus in the dirt,
      keening uncontrollably,
lurching forward in a hideous, electric dance as though someone were
      at him with a club.
When at last he'd finish, she'd wipe him with a tissue like a child; he'd
      lick her hand.
It was horrifying; I was always going to call the police; once I actually
      went out to chastise her—
didn't she know how selfish she was, how the animal was suffering?—
      she scared me off, though.
She was older than I'd thought, for one thing, her flesh was loosening,
      pouches of fat beneath the eyes,
and poorer, too, shabby, tarnished: I imagined smelling something faintly
      acrid as I passed.
Had I ever really mooned for such a creature? I slunk around the block,
      chagrined, abashed.
I don't recall them too long after that. Maybe the dog died, maybe I was
      just less sensitive.
Maybe one year when the cold came and I closed my windows, I forgot
      them . . . then I moved.
Everything was complicated now, so many tensions, so much bothersome
      self-consciousness.
Anyway, those back streets, especially in bad weather when the ginkgos
      lost their leaves, were bleak.
It's restored there now, ivy, pointed brick, garden walls with broken bottles
      mortared on them,
but you'd get sick and tired then: the rubbish in the gutter, the general
      sense of dereliction.
Also, I'd found a girl to be in love with: all we wanted was to live together,
      so we did.

The Gift

I have found what pleases my friend's chubby, rosy, gloriously shining-
   eyed year-old daughter.
She chirps, flirts with me, pulls herself up by my pants leg, and her
   pleasure is that I lift her,
high, by her thighs, over my head, and then that I let her suddenly fall,
   plunge, plummet,
down through my hands, to be, at the last instant, under the arms, in
   mid-gasp, caught.
She laughs when I do it, she giggles, roars; she is flushed with it, glowing,
   elated, ecstatic.
When I put her down, she whines, whimpers, claws at my lap: *Again*,
   she is saying . . . *Again: More.*
I pick up my glass, though, my friend and I chat, the child keeps at me
   but I pay no mind.

Once I would never have done that, released her like that, not until,
   satisfied, sated,
no need left, no "more," nothing would have been left for her but to
   fold sighing in my arms.
Once it was crucial that I be able to think of myself as unusually gifted
   with children.
And, even discounting the effort I put in it all, the premeditation, the
   scheming, I was.
I'd studied what they would want—at this age to rise, to fall, be tickled,
   caressed.
Older, to be heeded, attended: I had stories, dreams, ways to confide,
   take confidence back.
But beyond that, children did love me, I think, and beyond that, there
   seemed more.

I could calm crying babies, even when they were furious, shrieking, the
   mothers at wit's end.

88

I had rituals I'd devised, whisperings, clicks; soft, blowy whistles, a song-
voice.
A certain firmness of hand, I remember I thought: concentration, a
deepening of the gaze.
Maybe they'd be surprised to find me with them at all instead of the
mother or father,
but, always, they'd stop, sometimes so abruptly, with such drama, that
even I would be taken aback.
Tears, sometimes, would come to my eyes: I would be flooded with
thanks that I'd been endowed with this,
or had resurrected it from some primitive source of grace I imagined we'd
bartered away.

What else did I have then? Not very much: being alone most of the time,
retrospectively noble,
but bitter back then, brutal, abrasive, corrosive—I was wearing away with
it like a tooth.
And my sexual hunger, how a breast could destroy me, or a haunch: not
having the beautiful haunch.
. . . And love, too, I suppose, yes, now and then, for a girl, never for
other men's wives yet . . .
Where did the children fit in, though, that odd want to entrance and
enchant, to give bliss?
Did no one think I was mad? Didn't I ever wonder myself if I was using
the children,
whether needs or compulsions, at least sublimations, were unaccounted
for in my passion?

No, never, more sense to ask if those vulnerable creatures of the heart
used me.
The children were light—I thought they pertained to my wish to be pure,
a saint.
I never conjoined them with anything else, not with the loneliness or
the vile desire,
not with my rages nor the weary, nearly irrepressible urges I'd feel to let
go, to die.

The children were light, or let intimations of light through—they were
      the way to the soul:
I wanted to think myself, too, a matrix of innocent warmth instead of
      the sorrowing brute I was,
stumbling out by myself into the moaning darkness again, thrust again
      into that murderous prowl.

On Learning of a Friend's Illness

for James Wright

The morning is so gray that the grass is gray and the side of the white
    horse grazing
is as gray and hard as the harsh, insistent wind gnawing the iron surface
    of the river,
while far off on the other shore, the eruptions from the city seem for
    once more docile and benign
than the cover of nearly indistinguishable clouds they unfurl to insinuate
    themselves among.

It is a long while since the issues of mortality have taken me this way.
    Shivering,
I tramp the thin, bitten track to the first rise, the first descent, and, toiling
    up again,
I startle out of their brushy hollow the whole herd of wild-eyed, shaggy,
    unkempt mares,
their necks, rumps, withers, even faces begrimed with patches of the
    gluey, alluvial mud.

All of them at once, their nostrils flared, their tails flung up over their
    backs like flags,
are suddenly in flight, plunging and shoving along the narrow furrow of
    the flood ditch,
bursting from its mouth, charging headlong towards the wires at the
    pasture's end,
banking finally like one great, graceful wing to scatter down the hillside
    out of sight.

Only the oldest of them all stays with me, and she, sway-backed, over
    at the knees,
blind, most likely deaf, still, when I move towards her, swings her meager
    backside to me,
her ears flattening, the imperturbable opals of her eyes gazing resolutely
    over the bare,

91

scruffy fields, the scattered pines and stands of third-growth oak I called
a forest once.

I slip up on her, hook her narrow neck, haul her to me, hold her for a
moment, let her go.
I hardly can remember anymore what there ever was out here that keeps
me coming back
to watch the land be amputated by freeways and developments, and the
mares, in their sanctuary,
thinning out, reverting, becoming less and less approachable, more and
more the symbols of themselves.

How cold it is. The hoofprints in the hardened muck are frozen lakes,
their rims atilt,
their glazed opacities skewered with straw, muddled with the ancient and
ubiquitous manure.
I pick a morsel of it up: scentless, harmless, cool, as desiccated as an
empty hive,
it crumbles in my hand, its weightless, wingless filaments taken from me
by the wind and strewn

in a long, surprising arc that wavers once then seems to burst into a rain
of dust.
No comfort here, nothing to say, to try to say, nothing for anyone. I start
the long trek back,
the horses nowhere to be seen, the old one plodding wearily away to join
them,
the river, bitter to look at, and the passionless earth, and the grasses
rushing ceaselessly in place.

Combat

Ich hatte einst ein schönes Vaterland . . . Es war ein Traum.
—HEINRICH HEINE

I've been trying for hours to figure out who I was reminded of by the
welterweight fighter
I saw on television this afternoon all but ruin his opponent with coun-
terpunches and now I have it.
It was a girl I knew once, a woman: when he was being interviewed after
the knockout, he was her exactly,
the same rigorous carriage, same facial structure—sharp cheekbones, very
vivid eyebrows—
even the sheen of perspiration—that's how I'd remember her, of course
. . . Moira was her name—
and the same quality in the expression of unabashed self-involvement,
softened at once with a grave,
almost oversensitive attentiveness to saying with absolute precision what
was to be said.
Lovely Moira! Could I ever have forgotten you? No, not forgotten, only
not had with me for a time
that dark, slow voice, those vulnerable eyes, those ankles finely tendoned
as a thoroughbred's.
We met I don't remember where—everything that mattered happened
in her apartment, in the living room,
with her mother, whom she lived with, watching us, and in Moira's
bedroom down the book-lined corridor.
The mother, I remember, was so white, not all that old but white:
everything, hair, skin, lips, was ash,
except her feet, which Moira would often hold on her lap to massage
and which were a deep,
frightening yellow, the skin thickened and dense, horned with calluses
and chains of coarse, dry bunions,
the nails deformed and brown, so deeply buried that they looked like
chips of tortoiseshell.
Moira would rub the poor, sad things, twisting and kneading at them
with her strong hands;

the mother's eyes would be closed, occasionally she'd mutter something
under her breath in German.
That was their language—they were, Moira said, refugees, but the word
didn't do them justice.
They were well-off, very much so, their apartment was, in fact, the most
splendid thing I'd ever seen.
There were lithographs and etchings—some Klees, I think; a Munch—
a lot of very flat oriental rugs,
voluptuous leather furniture and china so frail the molds were surely cast
from butterflies.
I never found out how they'd brought it all with them: what Moira told
me was of displaced-person camps,
a pilgrimage on foot from Prussia and the Russians, then Frankfurt,
Rotterdam, and here, "freedom."
The trip across the war was a complicated memory for her; she'd been
very young, just in school,
what was most important to her at that age was her father, whom she'd
hardly known and who'd just died.
He was a general, she told me, the chief of staff or something of "the
war against the Russians."
He'd been one of the conspirators against Hitler and when the plot failed
he'd committed suicide,
all of which meant not very much to me, however good the story was
(and I heard it often),
because people then were still trying to forget the war, it had been almost
ignored, even in school,
and I had no context much beyond what my childhood comic books had
given me to hang any of it on.
Moira was fascinated by it, though, and by their journey, and whenever
she wanted to offer me something—
when I'd despair, for instance, of ever having from her what I had to
have—it would be, again, that tale.
In some ways it was, I think, her most precious possession, and every
time she'd unfold it
she'd seem to have forgotten having told me before: each time the images
would be the same—
a body by the roadside, a child's—awful—her mother'd tried to hide her
eyes but she'd jerked free;

94

a white ceramic cup of sweet, cold milk in the dingy railroad station of
      some forgotten city,
then the boat, the water, black, the webs of rushing foam she'd made
      up creatures for, who ran beneath the waves
and whose occupation was to snare the boat, to snarl it, then . . . she
      didn't know what then,
and I'd be hardly listening anyway by then, one hand on a thigh, the
      other stroking,
with such compassion, such generous concern, such cunning twenty-
      one-year-old commiseration,
her hair, her perfect hair, then the corner of her mouth, then, so far
      away, the rich rim of a breast.
We'd touch that way—petting was the word then—like lovers, with the
      mother right there with us,
probably, I remember thinking, because we weren't lovers, not really,
      not *that* way (not yet, I'd think),
but beyond that there seemed something else, some complicity between
      them, some very adult undertaking
that I sensed but couldn't understand and that astonished me as did almost
      everything about them.
I never really liked the mother—I was never given anything to like—but
      I was awed by her.
If I was left alone with her—Moira on the phone, say—I stuttered, or
      was stricken mute.
It felt like I was sitting there with time itself: everything seemed somehow
      finished for her,
but there seemed, still, to be such depths, or such ascensions, to her
      unblinking brooding.
She was like a footnote to a text, she seemed to know it, suffer it, and,
      if I was wildly uneasy with her,
my eyes battering shyly in their chutes, it was my own lack, my own
      unworthiness that made it so.
Moira would come back, we'd talk again, I can't imagine what about
      except, again, obsessively, the father,
his dying, his estates, the stables, servants, all they'd given up for the
      madness of that creature Hitler.
I'd listen to it all again, and drift, looking in her eyes, and pine, pondering
      her lips.

I knew that I was dying of desire—down of cheek; subtle, alien scent—
that I'd never felt desire like this.
I was so distracted that I couldn't even get their name right: they'd kept
the real pronunciation,
I'd try to ape what I remembered of my grandmother's Polish Yiddish
but it still eluded me
and Moira's little joke before she'd let me take her clothes off was that
we'd have lessons, "Von C . . ." "No, Von C . . ."
Later, when I was studying the holocaust, I found it again, the name,
Von C . . . , in Shirer's *Reich*:
it had, indeed, existed, and it had, yes, somewhere on the Eastern front,
blown its noble head off.
I wasn't very moved. I wasn't in that city anymore, I'd ceased long before
ever to see them,
and besides, I'd changed by then—I was more aware of history and was
beginning to realize,
however tardily, that one's moral structures tended to be air unless you
grounded them in real events.
Everything I did learn seemed to negate something else, everything was
more or less up for grabs,
but the war, the Germans, all I knew about that now—no, never: what
a complex triumph to have a nation,
all of it, beneath you, what a splendid culmination for the adolescence
of one's ethics!
As for Moira, as for her mother, what recompense for those awful hours,
those ecstatic unaccomplishments.
I reformulated her—them—forgave them, held them fondly, with a
heavy lick of condescension, in my system.
But for now, there we are, Moira and I, down that hall again, in her
room again, both with nothing on.
I can't say what she looked like. I remember that I thought her somewhat
too robust, her chest too thick,
but I was young, and terrified, and quibbled everything: now, no doubt,
I'd find her perfect.
In my mind now, naked, she's almost too much so, too blond, too gold,
her pubic hair, her arm and leg fur,
all of it is brushed with light, so much glare she seems to singe the very
tissue of remembrance,

but there are—I can see them now and didn't then—promises of dimness,
vaults and hidden banks of coolness.
If I couldn't, though, appreciate the subtleties, it wasn't going to hold
me back, no, it was *she* who held me back,
always, as we struggled on that narrow bed, twisted on each other, mauling
one another like demented athletes.
So fierce it was, so strenuous, aggressive: my thigh *here*, my hand *here*,
lips *here*, *here*,
hers *here* and *here* but never *there* or *there* . . . before it ended, she'd
have even gone into the sounds of love,
groans and whispered shrieks, glottal stops, gutturals I couldn't catch or
understand,
and all this while *nothing would be happening*, nothing, that is, in the
way I'd mean it now.
We'd lie back (this is where I see her sweating, gleaming with it, drenched)
and she'd smile.
She is satisfied somehow. This is what she wanted somehow. Only this?
Yes, only this,
and we'd be back, that quickly, in my recollection anyway, with the
mother in the other room,
the three of us in place, the conversation that seemed sometimes like a
ritual, eternally recurring.
How long we were to wait like this was never clear to me; my desperation,
though, was slow in gathering.
I must have liked the role, or the pretense of the role, of beast, primed,
about to pounce,
and besides, her hesitations, her fendings-off, were so warm and so
bewildering,
I was so engrossed in them, that when at last, once and for all, she let
me go,
the dismissal was so adroitly managed that I never realized until perhaps
right now
that what had happened wasn't my own coming to the conclusion that
this wasn't worth the bother.
It's strange now, doing it again, the business of the camps and slaughters,
the quick flicker of outrage
that hardly does its work anymore, all the carnage, all our own omissions
interposed,

97

then those two, in their chambers, correct, aristocratic, even with the
old one's calcifying feet
and the younger one's intensities—those eyes that pierce me still from
that far back with jolts of longing.
I frame the image: the two women, the young man, they, poised, gracious,
he smoldering with impatience,
and I realize I've never really asked myself what could she, or they,
possibly have wanted of me?
What am I doing in that room, a teacup trembling on my knee, that
odd, barbed name mangled in my mouth?
If she felt a real affinity or anything resembling it for me, it must have
been as something quaint—
young poet, brutish, or trying to be brutish—but no, I wasn't even that,
I was just a boy, harmless, awkward,
mildly appealing in some ways, I suppose, but certainly with not a thing
about me one could call compelling,
not compared to what, given her beauty and her means, she could have
had and very well may have, for all I knew.
What I come to now, running over it again, I think I want to keep as
undramatic as I can.
These revisions of the past are probably even less trustworthy than our
random, everyday assemblages
and have most likely even more to do with present unknowables, so I
offer this almost in passing,
with nothing, no moral distillation, no headily pressing imperatives meant
to be lurking beneath it.
I wonder, putting it most simply, leaving out humiliation, anything like
that, if I might have been their Jew?
I wonder, I mean, if I might have been an implement for them, not of
atonement—I'd have nosed that out—
but of absolution, what they'd have used to get them shed of something
rankling—history, it would be:
they'd have wanted to be categorically and finally shriven of it, or of that
part of it at least
which so befouled the rest, which so acutely contradicted it with glory
and debasement.
The mother, what I felt from her, that bulk of silence, that withholding
that I read as sorrow:

might it have been instead the heroic containment of a probably reflexive
loathing of me?
How much, no matter what their good intentions (of which from her I
had no evidence at all)
and even with the liberal husband (although the generals' reasons weren't
that pure and got there very late),
how much must they have inevitably absorbed, that Nazi generation,
those Aryan epochs?
And if the mother shuddered, what would Moira have gone through with
me spinning at her nipple,
her own juices and the inept emissions I'd splatter on her gluing her to
me?
The purifying Jew. It's almost funny. She was taking just enough of me
to lave her conscience,
and I, so earnest in my wants, blindly labored for her, dismantling guilt
or racial squeamishness
or whatever it was the refined tablet of her consciousness deemed it needed
to be stricken of.
All the indignities I let be perpetrated on me while I lolled in that
luxurious detention:
could I really have believed they only had to do with virtue, maidenhood,
or even with, I remember thinking—
I came this close—some intricate attempt Moira might be making to
redeem a slight on the part of the mother?
Or might inklings have arisen and might I, in my infatuation, have gone
along with them anyway?
I knew something, surely: I'd have had to. What I really knew, of course,
I'll never know again.
Beautiful memory, most precious and most treacherous sister: what tem-
ples must we build for you.
And even then, how belatedly you open to us; even then, with what
exuberance you cross us.

Floor

A dirty picture, a photograph, possibly a tintype, from the turn of the
    century, even before:
the woman is obese, gigantic; a broad, black corset cuts from under her
    breasts to the top of her hips,
her hair is crimped, wiry, fastened demurely back with a bow one in-
    congruous wing of which shows.
Her eyebrows are straight and heavy, emphasizing her frank, unintro-
    spective plainness
and she looks directly, easily into the camera, her expression somewhere
    between play and scorn,
as though the activities of the photographer were ridiculous or beneath
    her contempt, or,
rather, as though the unfamiliar camera were actually the much more
    interesting presence here
and how absurd it is that the lens be turned toward her and her partner
    and not back on itself.
One sees the same look—pride, for some reason, is in it, and a surprisingly
    sophisticated self-distancing—
in the snaps anthropologists took in backwaters during those first, polit-
    ically preconscious,
golden days of culture-hopping, and, as Goffman notes, in certain ad-
    vertisements, now.

The man is younger than the woman. Standing, he wears what looks
    like a bathing costume,
black-and-white tank top, heavy trousers bunched in an ungainly heap
    over his shoes, which are still on.
He has an immigrant's mustache he's a year or two too callow for, but,
    thick and dark, it will fit him.
He doesn't, like the woman, watch the camera, but stares ahead, not at
    the woman but slightly over and past,
and there's a kind of withdrawn, almost vulnerable thoughtfulness or
    preoccupation about him

despite the gross thighs cast on his waist and the awkward, surely both-
        ersome twist
his body has been forced to assume to more clearly exhibit the genital
        penetration.
He seems, in fact, abstracted—oblivious wouldn't be too strong a word
        —as though, possibly,
as unlikely as it would seem, he had been a virgin until now and was
        trying amid all this unholy confusion—
the hooded figure, the black box with its eye—trying, and from the looks
        of it even succeeding
in obliterating everything from his consciousness but the thing itself, the
        act itself,
so as, one would hope, to redeem the doubtlessly endless nights of the
        long Victorian adolescence.

The background is a painted screen: ivy, columns, clouds; some muse
        or grace or other,
heavy-buttocked, whory, flaunts her gauze and clodhops with a half-
        demented leer.
The whole thing's oddly poignant somehow, almost, like an antique
        wedding picture, comforting—
the past is sending out a tendril to us: poses, attitudes of stillness we've
        lost or given back.
Also, there's no shame in watching them, in being in the tacit commerce
        of having, like it or not,
received the business in one's hand, no titillation either, not a tangle,
        not a throb,
probably because the woman offers none of the normal symptoms, even
        if minimal, even if contrived—
the tongue, say, wandering from the corner of the mouth, a glint of extra
        brilliance at the lash—
we associate to even the most innocuous, undramatic, parental sorts of
        passion, and the boy,
well, dragged in out of history, off Broome or South Street, all he is is
        grandpa:
he'll go back into whatever hole he's found to camp in, those higher-
        contrast tenements

with their rows of rank, forbidding beds, or not even beds, rags on a
    floor, or floor.
On the way there, there'll be policemen breaking strikers' heads, or micks',
    or sheenies',
there'll be war somewhere, in the sweatshops girls will turn to stone over
    their Singers.
Here, at least peace. Here, one might imagine, after he withdraws, a
    kind of manly focus taking him—
the glance he shoots to her is hard and sure—and, to her, a tenderness
    might come,
she might reach a hand—Sweet Prince—to touch his cheek, or might
    —who can understand these things?—
avert her face and pull him to her for a time before she squats to flush
    him out.

Waking Jed

Deep asleep, perfect immobility, no apparent evidence of consciousness
    or of dream.
Elbow cocked, fist on pillow lightly curled to the tension of the partially
    relaxing sinew.
Head angled off, just so: the jaw's projection exaggerated slightly, almost
    to prognathous: why?
The features express nothing whatsoever and seem to call up no response
    in me.
Though I say nothing, don't move, gradually, far down within, he, or
    rather not *he* yet,
something, a presence, an element of being, becomes aware of me: there
    begins a subtle,
very gentle alteration in the structure of the face, or maybe less than
    that, more elusive,
as though the soft distortions of sleep-warmth radiating from his face and
    flesh,
those essentially unreal mirages in the air between us, were modifying,
    dissipating.
The face is now more his, Jed's—its participation in the almost Roman-
    esque generality
I wouldn't a moment ago have been quite able to specify, not having its
    contrary, diminishes.
Particularly on the cheekbones and chin, the skin is thinning, growing
    denser, harder,
the molecules on the points of bone coming to attention, the eyelids
    finer, brighter, foil-like:
capillaries, veins; though nothing moves, there are goings to and fro
    behind now.
One hand opens, closes down more tightly, the arm extends suddenly
    full-length,
jerks once at the end, again, holds: there's a more pronounced elongation
    of the skull—
the infant pudginess, whatever atavism it represented, or reversion, has
    been called back.

Now I sense, although I can't say how, his awareness of me: I can feel
    him begin to *think*,
I even know that he's thinking—or thinking in a dream perhaps—of me
    here watching him.
Now I'm aware—again, with no notion how, nothing indicates it—that
    if there was a dream,
it's gone, and, yes, his eyes abruptly open although his gaze, straight
    before him,
seems not to register just yet, the mental operations still independent of
    his vision.
I say his name, the way we do it, softly, calling one another from a cove
    or cave,
as though something else were there with us, not to be disturbed, to be
    crept along beside.
The lids come down again, he yawns, widely, very consciously mani-
    festing intentionality.
Great, if rudimentary, pleasure now: a sort of primitive, peculiarly mam-
    malian luxury—
to know, to know wonderfully that lying here, warm, protected, eyes
    closed, one can,
for a moment anyway, a precious instant, put off the lower-specie onsets,
    duties, debts.
Sleeker, somehow, slyer, more aggressive now, he is suddenly more
    awake, all awake,
already plotting, scheming, fending off: nothing said but there is mild
    rebellion, conflict:
I insist, he resists, and then, with abrupt, wriggling grace, he otters down
    from sight,
just his brow and crown, his shining rumpled hair, left ineptly showing
    from the sheet.
Which I pull back to find him in what he must believe a parody of sleep,
    himself asleep:
fetal, rigid, his arms clamped to his sides, eyes screwed shut, mouth
    clenched, grinning.

Neglect

An old hill town in northern Pennsylvania, a missed connection for a
    bus, an hour to kill.
For all intents and purposes, the place was uninhabited; the mines had
    closed years before—
anthracite too dear to dig, the companies went west to strip, the miners
    to the cities—
and now, although the four-lane truck route still went through—
    eighteen-wheelers pounding past—
that was almost all: a shuttered Buick dealer, a grocery, not even a
    McDonald's,
just the combination ticket office, luncheonette and five-and-dime where
    the buses turned around.
A low gray frame building, it was gloomy and rundown, but charmingly
    old-fashioned:
ancient wooden floors, open shelves, the smell of unwrapped candy,
    cigarettes and band-aid glue.
The only people there, the only people I think that I remember from
    the town at all,
were the silent woman at the register and a youngish teen-aged boy
    standing reading.
The woman smoked and smoked, stared out the streaky window, handed
    me my coffee with indifference.
It was hard to tell how old she was: her hair was dyed and teased, iced
    into a beehive.
The boy was frail, sidelong somehow, afflicted with a devastating Nessus-
    shirt of acne
boiling down his face and neck—pits and pores, scarlet streaks and scars;
    saddening.
We stood together at the magazine rack for a while before I realized what
    he was looking at.
Pornography: two naked men, one grimaces, the other, with a fist inside
    the first one, grins.

I must have flinched: the boy sidled down, blanked his face more and I
    left to take a walk.
It was cold, but not enough to catch or clear your breath: uncertain
    clouds, unemphatic light.
Everything seemed dimmed and colorless, the sense of surfaces dissolving,
    like the Parthenon.
Farther down the main street were a dentist and a chiropractor, both
    with hand-carved signs,
then the Elks' decaying clapboard mansion with a parking space "Reserved
    for the Exalted Ruler,"
and a Russian church, gilt onion domes, a four-horned air-raid siren on
    a pole between them.
Two blocks in, the old slate sidewalks shatter and uplift—gnawed lawns,
    aluminum butane tanks—
then the roads begin to peter out and rise: half-fenced yards with scabs
    of weeks-old snow,
thin, inky, oily leaks of melt insinuating down the gulleys and the cindered
    cuts
that rose again into the footings of the filthy, disused slagheaps ringing
    the horizon.
There was nowhere else. At the depot now, the woman and the boy were
    both behind the counter.
He was on a stool, his eyes closed, she stood just in back of him, massaging
    him,
hauling at his shoulders, kneading at the muscles like a boxer's trainer
    between rounds.
I picked up the county paper: it was anti-crime and welfare bums, for
    Reaganomics and defense.
The wire-photo was an actress in her swimming suit, that famously
    expensive bosom, cream.
My bus arrived at last, its heavy, healthy white exhaust pouring in the
    afternoon.
Glancing back, I felt a qualm, concern, an ill heart, almost parental,
    but before I'd hit the step,
the boy'd begun to blur, to look like someone else, the woman had
    already faded absolutely.

All that held now was that violated, looted country, the fraying fringes
       of the town,
those gutted hills, hills by rote, hills by permission, great, naked wastes
       of wrack and spill,
vivid and disconsolate, like genitalia shaved and disinfected for an op-
       eration.

The Regulars

In the Colonial Luncheonette on Sixth Street they know everything there
    is to know, the shits.
Sam Terminadi will tell you how to gamble yourself at age sixty from
    accountant to bookie,
and Sam Finkel will tell you more than anyone cares to hear how to
    parlay an ulcer into a pension
so you can sit here drinking this shit coffee and eating these overfried
    shit eggs
while you explain that the reasons the people across the street are going
    to go bust
in the toy store they're redoing the old fish market into—the father and
    son plastering,
putting up shelves, scraping the floors; the mother laboring over the white
    paint,
even the daughter coming from school to mop the century of scales and
    splatter from the cellar—
are both simple and complex because Sam T can tell you the answer to
    anything in the world
in one word and Sam F prefaces all his I-told-you-so's with "You don't
    understand, it's complex."
"It's simple," Sam T says, "where around here is anyone going to get
    money for toys?" The end.
Never mind the neighborhood's changing so fast that the new houses at
    the end of the block
are selling for twice what the whole block would have five years ago,
    that's not the point.
Business shits, right? Besides, the family—what's that they're eating?—
    are wrong, right?
Not totally wrong, what are they, Arabs or something? but still, wrong
    enough, that's sure.
"And where do they live?" Sam F asks. "Sure as shit their last dime's in
    the lease and shit sure
they'll end up living in back of the store like gypsies, guaranteed: didn't
    I tell you or not

when the Minskys were still here that they'd bug out first chance they
     got, and did they or no?"
Everyone thought the Minsky brothers would finally get driven out of
     their auto repair shop
by zoning or by having their tools stolen so many times, Once, Frank
     Minsky would growl,
on Yom Kippur, for crying out loud, but no, at the end, they just sold,
     they'd worked fifty years,
And Shit, Frank said, that's fucking enough, we're going to Miami, what
     do you want from me?
But Sam F still holds it against them, to cave in like that, the buggers,
     bastards, shits . . .
What he really means, Sam, Sam, is that everyone misses the Minskys'
     back room, where they'd head,
come dusk, the old boys, and there'd be the bottle of schnapps and the
     tits from *Playboy*
in the grimy half-dark with the good stink of three lifetimes of grease and
     sweat and bitching,
and how good that would be, back then, oh, how far back was then?
     Last year, is that all?
"They got no class: shit, a toy store," Sam T says. What does that mean,
     Sam? What class?
No class, that's all, simple: six months there and boom, they'll have a
     fire, guaranteed.
Poor Sam, whether the last fire, at the only butcher store for blocks the
     A&P hadn't swallowed,
was arson for insurance as Sam proved the next day, or whether, the way
     the firemen saw it,
it was just a bum keeping warm in the alley, Sam's decided to take it
     out on the strangers,
glaring at them over there in their store of dreams, their damned pain-
     in-the-ass toy store.
What's the matter with you, are you crazy? is what the father finally
     storms in with one afternoon,
both Sams turning their backs, back to their shit burgers, but old Bernie
     himself is working today,
and *Hey*, Bernie says, *Don't mind them, they're just old shits, sit down,*
     I'll buy you a coffee.

Who the fuck do they think they are? Here have a donut, don't worry,
     they'll be all right,
and of course they will be. "In a month you won't get them out of your
     hair," says Bernie,
and he's right again, old Bernie, before you know it Sam T has got me
     cornered in the street.
"What is it, for Christ's sake, Sam? Let me go." "No, wait up, it's a
     computer for kids."
"Sam, please, I'm in a hurry." "No, hold on, just a second, look, it's
     simple."

The Gas Station

This is before I'd read Nietzsche. Before Kant or Kierkegaard, even before
    Whitman and Yeats.
I don't think there were three words in my head yet. I knew, perhaps,
    that I should suffer,
I can remember I almost cried for this or for that, nothing special, nothing
    to speak of.
Probably I was mad with grief for the loss of my childhood, but I wouldn't
    have known that.
It's dawn. A gas station. Route twenty-two. I remember exactly: route
    twenty-two curved,
there was a squat, striped concrete divider they'd put in after a plague of
    collisions.
The gas station? Texaco, Esso—I don't know. They were just words
    anyway then, just what their signs said.
I wouldn't have understood the first thing about monopoly or imperialist
    or oppression.
It's dawn. It's so late. Even then, when I was never tired, I'm just holding
    on.
Slumped on my friend's shoulder, I watch the relentless, wordless misery
    of the route twenty-two sky
that seems to be filming my face with a grainy oil I keep trying to rub
    off or in.
Why are we here? Because one of my friends, in the men's room over
    there, has blue balls.
He has to jerk off. I don't know what that means, "blue balls," or why
    he has to do that—
it must be important to have to stop here after this long night, but I don't
    ask.
I'm just trying, I think, to keep my head as empty as I can for as long
    as I can.
One of my other friends is asleep. He's so ugly, his mouth hanging, slack
    and wet.
Another—I'll never see this one again—stares from the window as though
    he were frightened.

Here's what we've done. We were in Times Square, a pimp found us,
    corralled us, led us somewhere,
down a dark street, another dark street, up dark stairs, dark hall, dark
    apartment,
where his whore, his girl or his wife or his mother for all I know, dragged
    herself from her sleep,
propped herself on an elbow, gazed into the dark hall, and agreed, for
    two dollars each, to take care of us.
Take care of us. Some of the words that come through me now seem to
    stay, to hook in.
My friend in the bathroom is taking so long. The filthy sky must be
    starting to lighten.
It took me a long time, too, with the woman, I mean. Did I mention
    that she, the woman, the whore or mother,
was having her time and all she would deign do was to blow us? Did I
    say that? Deign? Blow?
What a joy, though, the idea was in those days. Blown! What a thing
    to tell the next day.
She only deigned, though, no more. She was like a machine. When I
    lift her back to me now,
there's nothing there but that dark, curly head, working, a machine, up
    and down, and now,
Freud, Marx, Fathers, tell me, what am I, doing this, telling this, on
    her, on myself,
hammering it down, cementing it, sealing it in, but a machine, too?
    Why am I doing this?
I still haven't read Augustine. I don't understand Chomsky that well.
    Should I?
My friend at last comes back. Maybe the right words were there all along.
    Complicity. Wonder.
How pure we were then, before Rimbaud, before Blake. *Grace. Love.*
    Take care of us. Please.

Tar

The first morning of Three Mile Island: those first disquieting, uncertain,
    mystifying hours.
All morning a crew of workmen have been tearing the old decrepit roof
    off our building,
and all morning, trying to distract myself, I've been wandering out to
    watch them
as they hack away the leaden layers of asbestos paper and disassemble
    the disintegrating drains.
After half a night of listening to the news, wondering how to know a
    hundred miles downwind
if and when to make a run for it and where, then a coming bolt awake
    at seven
when the roofers we've been waiting for since winter sent their ladders
    shrieking up our wall,
we still know less than nothing: the utility company continues making
    little of the accident,
the slick federal spokesmen still have their evasions in some semblance
    of order.
Surely we suspect now we're being lied to, but in the meantime, there
    are the roofers,
setting winch-frames, sledging rounds of tar apart, and there I am, on
    the curb across, gawking.

I never realized what brutal work it is, how matter-of-factly and harrow-
    ingly dangerous.
The ladders flex and quiver, things skid from the edge, the materials are
    bulky and recalcitrant.
When the rusty, antique nails are levered out, their heads pull off; the
    underroofing crumbles.
Even the battered little furnace, roaring along as patient as a donkey,
    chokes and clogs,
a dense, malignant smoke shoots up, and someone has to fiddle with a
    cock, then hammer it,
before the gush and stench will deintensify, the dark, Dantean broth
    wearily subside.

113

In its crucible, the stuff looks bland, like licorice, spill it, though, on
     your boots or coveralls,
it sears, and everything is permeated with it, the furnace gunked with
     burst and half-burst bubbles,
the men themselves so completely slashed and mucked they seem almost
     from another realm, like trolls.
When they take their break, they leave their brooms standing at attention
     in the asphalt pails,
work gloves clinging like Br'er Rabbit to the bitten shafts, and they slouch
     along the precipitous lip,
the enormous sky behind them, the heavy noontime air alive with shim-
     mers and mirages.

Sometime in the afternoon I had to go inside: the advent of our vigil was
     upon us.
However much we didn't want to, however little we would do about it,
     we'd understood:
we were going to perish of all this, if not now, then soon, if not soon,
     then someday.
Someday, some final generation, hysterically aswarm beneath an at-
     mosphere as unrelenting as rock,
would rue us all, anathematize our earthly comforts, curse our surfeits
     and submissions.
I think I know, though I might rather not, why my roofers stay so clear
     to me and why the rest,
the terror of that time, the reflexive disbelief and distancing, all we should
     hold on to, dims so.
I remember the president in his absurd protective booties, looking
     absolutely unafraid, the fool.
I remember a woman on the front page glaring across the misty Sus-
     quehanna at those looming stacks.
But, more vividly, the men, silvered with glitter from the shingles, cling-
     ing like starlings beneath the eaves.
Even the leftover carats of tar in the gutter, so black they seemed to suck
     the light out of the air.
By nightfall kids had come across them: every sidewalk on the block was
     scribbled with obscenities and hearts.

FROM

Flesh and Blood

[1 9 8 7]

Elms

All morning the tree men have been taking down the stricken elms skirting
    the broad sidewalks.
The pitiless electric chain saws whine tirelessly up and down their pierc-
    ing, operatic scales
and the diesel choppers in the street shredding the debris chug feverishly,
    incessantly,
packing truckload after truckload with the feathery, homogenized, inert
    remains of heartwood,
twig and leaf and soon the block is stripped, it is as though illusions of
    reality were stripped:
the rows of naked facing buildings stare and think, their divagations more
    urgent than they were.
"The winds of time," they think, the mystery charged with fearful clarity:
    "The winds of time . . ."
All afternoon, on to the unhealing evening, minds racing, "Insolent,
    unconscionable, the winds of time . . ."

Hooks

Possibly because she's already so striking—tall, well dressed, very clear,
    pure skin—
when the girl gets on the subway at Lafayette Street everyone notices her
    artificial hand
but we also manage, as we almost always do, not to be noticed noticing,
    except one sleeping woman,
who hasn't budged since Brooklyn but who lifts her head now, opens up,
    forgets herself,
and frankly stares at those intimidating twists of steel, the homely leather
    sock and laces,
so that the girl, as she comes through the door, has to do in turn now
    what is to be done,
which is to look down at it, too, a bit askance, with an air of tolerant,
    bemused annoyance,
the way someone would glance at their unruly, apparently ferocious but
    really quite friendly dog.

Nostalgia

In the dumbest movie they can play it on us with a sunrise and a passage
    of adagio Vivaldi—
all the reason more to love it and to loathe it, this always barely choked-
    back luscious flood,
this turbulence in breast and breath that indicates a purity residing some-
    where in us,
redeeming with its easy access the thousand lapses of memory shed in
    the most innocuous day
and canceling our rue for all the greater consciousness we didn't have
    for past, lost presents.
Its illusion is that we'll retain this new, however hammy past more
    thoroughly than all before,
its reality, that though we know by heart its shabby ruses, know we'll
    misplace it yet again,
it's what we have, a stage light flickering to flood, chintz and gaud, and
    we don't care.

Guatemala: 1964

for Loren Crabtree

The Maya-Quechua Indians plodding to market on feet as flat and tough
    as toads were semi-starving
but we managed to notice only their brilliant weaving and implacable,
    picturesque aloofness.
The only people who would talk to us were the village alcoholic, who
    sold his soul for *aguardiente,*
and the Bahia nurse, Jenny, middle-aged, English-Nicaraguan, the sole
    medicine for eighty miles,
who lord knows why befriended us, put us up, even took us in her jeep
    into the mountains,
where a child, if I remember, needed penicillin, and where the groups
    of dark, idling men
who since have risen and been crushed noted us with something discon-
    certingly beyond suspicion.
Good Jenny: it took this long to understand she wasn't just forgiving our
    ferocious innocence.

Herakles

A mysterious didactic urgency informs the compelling bedtime stories he
  is obsessively recounted.
Misty, potent creatures, half-human, half-insane with hatred and with
  lustings for the hearth:
the childhood of the race, with always, as the ground, the urgent im-
  plication of a lesson.
Some of it he gets, that there are losses, personal and epic, but bearable,
  to be withstood,
and that the hero's soul is self-forged, self-conceived, hammered out in
  outrage, trial, abandon, risk.
The parables elude him, though: he can never quite grasp where the
  ever-after means to manifest.
Is he supposed to *be* this darkly tempered, dark fanatic of the flesh who'll
  surely consume himself?
Or should it be the opposite: would all these feats and deeds be not
  exemplary but cautionary?

First Desires

It was like listening to the record of a symphony before you knew anything
    at all about the music,
what the instruments might sound like, look like, what portion of the
    orchestra each represented:
there were only volumes and velocities, thickenings and thinnings, the
    winding cries of change
that seemed to touch within you, through your body, to be part of you
    and then apart from you.
And even when you'd learned the grainy timbre of the single violin, the
    ardent arpeggios of the horn,
when you tried again there were still uneases and confusions left, an
    ache, a sense of longing
that held you in chromatic dissonance, droning on beyond the dominant's
    resolve into the tonic,
as though there were a flaw of logic in the structure, or in (you knew it
    was more likely) you.

The Dirty Talker: D Line, Boston

Shabby, tweedy, academic, he was old enough to be her father and I
    thought he was her father,
then realized he was standing closer than a father would so I thought he
    was her older lover.
And I thought at first that she was laughing, then saw it was more serious,
    more strenuous:
her shoulders spasmed back and forth; he was leaning close, his mouth
    almost against her ear.
He's terminating the affair, I thought: wife ill, the kids . . . the girl won't
    let him go.
We were in a station now, he pulled back half a head from her the better
    to behold her,
then was out the hissing doors, she sobbing wholly now so that finally I
    had to understand—
her tears, his grinning broadly in—at *me* now though, as though I were
    a portion of the story.

Repression

More and more lately, as, not even minding the slippages yet, the aches
  and sad softenings,
I settle into my other years, I notice how many of what I once thought
  were evidences of repression,
sexual or otherwise, now seem, in other people anyway, to be varieties
  of dignity, withholding, tact,
and sometimes even in myself, certain patiences I would have once called
  lassitude, indifference,
now seem possibly to be if not the rewards then at least the unsuspected,
  undreamed-of conclusions
to many of the even-then-preposterous self-evolved disciplines, rigors,
  almost mortifications
I inflicted on myself in my starting-out days, improvement days, days
  when the idea alone of psychic peace,
of intellectual, of emotional quiet, the merest hint, would have meant
  inconceivable capitulation.

Alzheimer's: The Wife

for Renée Mauger

She answers the bothersome telephone, takes the message, forgets the
message, forgets who called.
One of their daughters, her husband guesses: the one with the dogs, the
babies, the boy Jed?
Yes, perhaps, but how tell which, how tell anything when all the name
tags have been lost or switched,
when all the lonely flowers of sense and memory bloom and die now in
adjacent bites of time?
Sometimes her own face will suddenly appear with terrifying inappro-
priateness before her in a mirror.
She knows that if she's patient, its gaze will break, demurely, decorously,
like a well-taught child's,
it will turn from her as though it were embarrassed by the secrets of this
awful hide-and-seek.
If she forgets, though, and glances back again, it will still be in there,
furtively watching, crying.

Alzheimer's: The Husband

for Jean Mauger

He'd been a clod, he knew, yes, always aiming toward his vision of the
    good life, always acting on it.
He knew he'd been unconscionably self-centered, had indulged himself
    with his undreamed-of good fortune,
but he also knew that the single-mindedness with which he'd attended
    to his passions, needs and whims,
and which must have seemed to others the grossest sort of egotism, was
    also what was really at the base
of how he'd almost offhandedly worked out the intuitions and moves
    which had brought him here,
and this wasn't all that different: to spend his long-anticipated retirement
    learning to cook,
clean house, dress her, even to apply her makeup, wasn't any sort of
    secular saintliness—
that would be belittling—it was just the next necessity he saw himself as
    being called to.

The Critic

In the Boston Public Library on Boylston Street, where all the bums
    come in stinking from the cold,
there was one who had a battered loose-leaf book he used to scribble in
    for hours on end.
He wrote with no apparent hesitation, quickly, and with concentration;
    his inspiration was inspiring:
you had to look again to realize that he was writing over words that were
    already there—
blocks of cursive etched into the softened paper, interspersed with poems
    in print he'd pasted in.
I hated to think of the volumes he'd violated to construct his opus, but
    I liked him anyway,
especially the way he'd often reach the end, close his work with weary
    satisfaction, then open again
and start again: page one, chapter one, his blood-rimmed eyes as rapt as
    David's doing psalms.

New Car

Doesn't, when we touch it, that sheen of infinitesimally pebbled steel,
    doesn't it, perhaps,
give just a bit, yes, the subtlest yielding, yes, much less than flesh would,
    we realize,
but still, as though it were intending in some formal way that at last we
    were to be in contact
with the world of inorganics, as though, after all we've been through
    with it, cuts, falls, blows,
that world, the realm of carbon, iron, earth, the all-ungiving, was at-
    tempting, gently, patiently,
to reach across, respond, and mightn't we find now, not to our horror
    or even our discomfort,
that our tongue, as though in answer, had wandered gently from the
    mouth, as though it, too,
shriven of its limits, bud and duct, would sanctify this unity, would
    touch, stroke, cling, fuse?

Conscience

In how many of the miserable little life dramas I play out in my mind
      am I unforgivable,
despicable, with everything, love, kin, companionship, negotiable, mar-
      ketable, for sale,
and yet I do forgive myself, hardly marking it, although I still remember
      those fierce
if innocently violent fantasies of my eternal adolescence which could
      nearly knock me down
and send me howling through myself for caves of simple silence, black-
      ness, oblivion.
The bubble hardens, the opacities perfected: no one in here anymore to
      bring accusation,
no sob of shame to catch us in its throat, no omniscient angel, either,
      poor angel, child,
tremulous, aghast, covering its eyes and ears, compulsively washing out
      its mouth with soap.

Drought

A species of thistle no one had ever seen before appeared almost overnight
    in all the meadows,
coarse, gray-greenish clumps scattered anywhere the dying grass had
    opened up bare earth.
The farmers knew better or were too weary to try to fight the things, but
    their children,
walking out beside them through the sunset down the hillsides toward
    the still cool woods
along the narrowed brooks, would kick the plants or try to pry them out
    with pointed sticks:
the tenacious roots would hardly ever want to give, though, and it was
    too hot still to do much more
than crouch together where the thick, lethargic water filtered up and ran
    a few uncertain feet,
moistening the pebbles, forming puddles where the thriving insects could
    repose and reproduce.

End of Drought

It is the opposite or so of the friendly gossip from upstairs who stops by
        every other evening.
It's the time she comes in once too often, or it's more exactly in the
        middle of her tête-à-tête,
when she grows tedious beyond belief, and you realize that unless an
        etiquette is violated
this will just go on forever, the way, forever, rain never comes, then
        comes, the luscious opposite,
the shock of early drops, the pavements and the rooftops drinking, then
        the scent, so heady with release
it's almost overwhelming, thick and vaginal, and then the earth, terrified
        that she'd bungled it,
that she'd dwelt too long upon the problems of the body and the mind,
        the ancient earth herself,
like someone finally touching pen to page, breathes her languid, aching
        suspiration of relief.

Easter

As though it were the very soul of rational human intercourse which had
    been violated,
I can't believe you did that, the father chokes out to his little son, kneeling
    beside him,
tugging at the waistband of the tiny blue jeans, peering in along the split
    between the buttocks,
putting down his face at last to sniff, then saying it again, with quiet
    indignation, outrage,
a power more moral than parental: at issue here are covenants, agreements
    from the dawn of time.
The child, meanwhile, his eyes a little wider than they might be, is
    otherwise unblinking;
all the time the father raves, he stares, scholarly, detached, at a package
    in his hands:
a box of foil-wrapped chocolate eggs, because it's spring, because the god
    has died, and risen.

Bishop Tutu's Visit to the White House: 1984

I am afraid for you a little, for your sense of shame; I feel you are
    accustomed to ordinary evil.
Your assumption will be that disagreeing with your methods, he will
    nevertheless grasp the problems.
You will assume that he will be involved, as all humans must be, for
    what else is it to be human,
in a notion of personal identity as a progress toward a more conscious,
    inclusive spiritual condition,
so that redemption, in whatever terms it might occur, categorically will
    have been earned.
How will you bear that for him and those around him, righteousness
    and self are *a priori* equal,
that to have stated one's good intentions excuses in advance from any
    painful sense of sin?
I fear you will be wounded by his obtuseness, humiliated by his pride,
    mortified by his absurd power.

Experience

After a string of failed romances and intensely remarked sexual adventures
   she'd finally married.
The husband was a very formal man, handsome, elegant . . . perhaps
   to my taste too much so;
I sensed too much commitment in him to a life entailing . . . hand-
   someness and elegance, I suppose,
but he was generous with her and even their frequent arguments had a
   manageable vehemence.
She smiled often in those days, but behind her face an edge of animation
   seemed nailed shut.
You wouldn't really worry for her, by now you knew she'd be all right,
   but there were moments
when for no reason you could put your finger on you'd feel something
   in yourself too rigidly attentive:
it was as though some soft herd-alarm, a warning signal from the species,
   had been permanently tripped.

Resentment

What is there which so approaches an art form in its stubborn patience,
    its devotion to technique,
to elegant refinement: that relentless searching for receptacles to capture
    content and expression?
The fiercest lust of self toward self: is there anything which keeps the
    soul so *occupied?*
My slights, affronts: how I shuffle and reshuffle them, file them, index,
    code, and collate.
Justification, accusation: I permutate, elaborate, combine, condense, re-
    focus, re-refine.
I mull, I ponder, convince, cajole; prove, disprove, accomplish, reac-
    complish, satisfy, solve.
Begin again: courageous, unflinching, resigned, my conscience swooning
    with projected ingenuities;
my mind's two mouths, their song, their kiss, this inaccomplishable,
    accomplished consummation!

Mornings: Catherine

Sometimes she'd begin to sing to herself before she was out of bed, before,
      I can remember thinking
as I listened from my table in the other room, she really could have even
      been all the way awake:
no sound of sheets pulled back, footsteps, just her voice, her song, so
      soft at first I wasn't sure,
rising from the silence but so close to being in it still that I couldn't hear
      the words,
only threads of melody a car passing or a child crying in another house
      would brush away,
until it would insist again, or I'd think it would, with the volume of a
      breeze, the odor of a breeze . . .
Waiting to hear it again, to hear her again, I wouldn't move, I'd almost,
      yes, hold my breath:
her voice, her song, the meshings and unmeshings with the attending
      world, with my incredulity.

War

Jed is breathlessly, deliriously happy because he's just been deftly am-
bushed and gunned down
by his friend Ha Woei as he came charging headlong around the corner
of some bushes in the *bois*.
He slumps dramatically to the ground, disregarding the damp, black,
gritty dirt he falls into,
and holds the posture of a dead man, forehead to the earth, arms and
legs thrown full-length east and west,
until it's time for him to rise and Ha Woei to die, which Ha Woei does
with vigor and abandon,
flinging himself down, the imaginary rifle catapulted from his hand like
Capa's Spanish soldier's.
Dinnertime, bath time, bedtime, story time: *bam, bambambam, bam*—
Akhilleus and Hektor.
Not until the cloak of night falls do they give themselves to the truces
and forgivenesses of sleep.

Greed

A much-beaten-upon-looking, bedraggled blackbird, not a starling, with
      a mangled or tumorous claw,
an extra-evil air, comically malignant, like something from a folktale
      meant to frighten you,
gimps his way over the picnic table to a cube of moist white cheese into
      which he drives his beak.
Then a glister of licentious leering, a conspiratorial gleam, the cocked
      brow of common avarice:
he works his yellow scissors deeper in, daring doubt, a politician with
      his finger in the till,
a weapon maker's finger in the politician, the slobber and the licking
      and the champ and click.
It is a lovely day, it always is; the innocent daylight fades into its dying,
      it always does.
The bird looks up, death-face beside the curded white, its foot, its fist of
      dying, daintily raised.

The Past

All along certainly it's been there, waiting before us, waiting to receive
    us, not to waver,
flickering shakily across the mind-screen, always in another shadow,
    always potentially illusion,
but out ahead, where it should be, redeemable, retrievable, accessible
    not by imagination's nets
but by the virtue of its being, simply being, waiting patiently for us like
    any other unattended,
any other hardly anticipated or not even anticipated—as much as any
    other fact rolling in . . .
All the project needs is patience, cunning, similar to that with which we
    outwit trembling death . . .
Not "history" but scent, sound, sight, the sensual fact, the beings and
    the doings, the heroes,
unmediated now, the holy and the horrid, to be worked across not like
    a wistful map, but land.

The Modern

Its skin tough and unpliable as scar, the pulp out of focus, weak, granular,
	powdery, blank,
this tomato I'm eating—wolfing, stuffing down: I'm so hungry—is hor-
	rible and delicious.
Don't tell me, I know all about it, this travesty-sham; I know it was
	plucked green and unripe,
then was locked in a chamber and gassed so it wouldn't rot till I bought
	it but I don't care:
I was so famished before, I was sucking sweat from my arm and now my
	tomato is glowing inside me.
I muscle the juice through my teeth and the seeds to the roof of my
	mouth and the hard,
scaly scab of where fruit met innocent stem and was torn free I hold on
	my tongue and savor,
a coin, a dot, the end of a sentence, the end of the long improbable
	utterance of the holy and human.

Failure

Maybe it's not as bad as we like to think: no melodramatic rendings,
  sackcloths, nothing so acute
as the fantasies of conscience chart in their uncontrollably self-punishing
  rigors and admonitions.
Less love, yes, but what was love: a febrile, restless, bothersome trembling
  to continue to possess
what one was only partly certain was worth wanting anyway, and if the
  reservoir of hope is depleted,
neither do distracting expectations interfere with these absorbing medi-
  tations on the frailties of chance.
A certain *resonance* might be all that lacks; the voice spinning out in
  darkness in an empty room.
The recompense is knowing that at last you've disconnected from the
  narratives that conditioned you
to want to be what you were never going to be, while here you are still
  this far from "the end."

Crime

John the tailor had gone racing up the stairs in back of his store and
  because he was so frightened
had jumped right out the window into the street where he broke his arm,
  though not badly.
A mounted policeman who'd been with his married girlfriend around
  the corner heard the shouts
and came cantering up just as the holdup man with a pistol in his hand
  was coming out:
the policeman pulled his gun, shot once, hit the robber in the chest,
  and it was over.
By the time I got there, everybody was waiting for the ambulance, John
  was still sobbing,
the crook was lying next to that amazing clot of blood, congealed to the
  consistency of cow plop,
and kids were darting from the crowd, scrambling for the change he'd
  let spill when he fell.

Fat

The young girl jogging in mittens and skimpy gym shorts through a
     freezing rainstorm up our block
would have a perfect centerfold body except for the bulbs of grandmotherly
     fat on her thighs.
Who was it again I loved once . . . no, not loved truly, liked, somewhat,
     and slept with, a lot,
who when she'd brood on the I thought quite adorable blubber she had
     there would beat it on the wall?
Really: she'd post herself naked half a stride back, crouch like a skier,
     and swing her hips, bang!
onto the plaster, bang! ten times, a hundred: bang! the wall shook, bang!
     her poor body quivered.
I'd lie there aghast, I knew that mad pounding had to mean more than
     itself, of course I thought me.
For once I was right; soon after, she left me, and guess what, for all that,
     I missed her.

Junior High School Concert: Salle Rossini

Each movement of the Mozart has a soloist and as each appears the
      conductor tunes her instrument,
while they, pubescent girls all, look fiercely unconcerned with being
      possibly made fools of.
Their teacher is oblivious to that, though with his graying dentures he
      seems kind enough,
he just loves music more—you can tell he might love music more than
      Toscanini or than Bach.
It might be the saddest thing about the arts that they so seldom recompense
      passion and commitment
with genius or with anything at all beyond a ground-floor competence,
      but *tant pis!* for that,
the old man seems to say, *Tant pis!* too if the cellos thump, if the *lento*
      is a trifle tired,
if the girl slogging through as soon would let the whole thing drop: *Tant
      pis!* everything: *Bravo!*

The Prodigy

for Elizabeth Bishop

Though no shyer than the others—while her pitch is being checked she
        beams out at the audience,
one ear sticking through her fine, straight, dark hair, Nabokov would
        sure say "deliciously"—
she's younger, slimmer, flatter, still almost a child: her bow looks half a
        foot too big for her.
Not when she begins to play, though: when she begins to play, when
        she goes swooping, leaping,
lifting from the lumbering *tutti* like a fighter plane, that bow is fire, that
        bow is song,
that bow lifts all of us, father and old uncle, yawning younger brother
        and bored best friend,
and brings us all to song, to more than song, to breaths breathed for us,
        sharp, indrawn,
and then, as she bows it higher and higher, to old sorrows redeemed, a
        sweet sensation of joy.

Souls

Bound with baling wire to the tubular jerry-built bumper of a beat-up
    old dump truck
are two of those gigantic teddy bears people win (usually shills) in cheap
    amusement parks.
It's pouring: dressed in real children's clothes, they are, our mothers
    would have said, drenched,
and they're also unrelentingly filthy, matted with the sticky, sickly,
    ghastly, dark gray sheen
you see on bums ambulating between drinking streets and on mongrels
    guarding junkyards.
Their stuffing hasn't been so crushed in them as to affect their jaunty,
    open-armed availability,
but, regarded more closely, they seem to manifest a fanatical expression-
    lessness, like soldiers,
who, wounded, captured, waiting to be shipped away or shot, must submit
    now to their photograph.

Fifteen

for Jessie

You give no hint how shy you really are, so thoroughly your warm and
    welcoming temperament masks
those confounding and to me still painful storms of adolescent ill at ease,
    confusion and disruption.
Our old father-daughter stroll down South Street these days is like a foray
    into the territories—
the weighings and the longings, young men, men of age, the brazen or
    sidelong subliminal proposings:
you're fair game now, but if you notice, you manage to keep it unim-
    peachably to yourself,
your newly braceless smile good-humoredly desexualizing the leering and
    licentious out-there.
Innocently you sheathe yourself in the most patently innocuous and
    unpremeditated innocence;
even with me, though, your kiss goodbye is layered: cheek towards, body
    swayed imperceptibly away.

Thinking Thought

"Oh, soul," I sometimes—often—still say when I'm trying to convince
   my inner self of something.
"Oh, soul," I say still, "there's so much to be done, don't want to stop
   to rest now, not already.
"Oh, soul," I say, "the implications of the task are clear, why procras-
   tinate, why whine?"
All the while I know my struggle has to do with mind being only some-
   times subject to the will,
that other portion of itself which manages to stay so recalcitrantly, ob-
   stinately impotent.
"Oh, soul, come into my field of want, my realm of act, be attentive to
   my computations and predictions."
But as usual soul resists, as usual soul retires, as usual soul's old act of
   dissipation and removal.
Oh, the furious illusive unities of want, the frail, false fusions and dis-
   cursive chains of hope.

Snow: I

All night, snow, then, near dawn, freezing rain, so that by morning the
    whole city glistens
in a glaze of high-pitched, meticulously polished brilliance, everything
    rounded off,
the cars submerged nearly to their windows in the unbroken drifts lining
    the narrow alleys,
the buildings rising from the trunklike integuments the wind has molded
    against them.
Underlit clouds, blurred, violet bars, the rearguard of the storm, still
    hang in the east,
immobile over the flat river basin of the Delaware; beyond them, nothing,
    the washed sky,
one vivid wisp of pale smoke rising waveringly but emphatically into the
    brilliant ether.
No one is out yet but Catherine, who closes the door behind her and
    starts up the street.

Snow: II

It's very cold, Catherine is bundled in a coat, a poncho on top of that,
high boots, gloves,
a long scarf around her neck, and she's sauntering up the middle of the
snowed-in street,
eating, of all things, an apple, the blazing redness of which shocks against
the world of white.
No traffic yet, the *crisp crisp* of her footsteps keeps reaching me until she
turns the corner.
I write it down years later, and the picture still holds perfectly, precise,
unwanting,
and so too does the sense of being suddenly bereft as she passes abruptly
from my sight,
the quick wash of desolation, the release again into the memory of af-
fection, and then affection,
as the first trucks blundered past, chains pounding, the first delighted
children rushed out with sleds.

Kin

"You make me sick!" this, with rancor, vehemence, disgust—again, "You
    hear me? *Sick!*"
with rancor, vehemence, disgust again, with rage and bitterness, arro-
    gance and fury—
from a little black girl, ten or so, one evening in a convenience market,
    to her sister,
two or three years younger, who's taking much too long picking out her
    candy from the rack.
What next? Nothing next. Next the wretched history of the world. The
    history of the heart.
The theory next that all we are are stories, handed down, that all we are
    are parts of speech.
All that limits and defines us: our ancient natures, love and death and
    terror and original sin.
And the weary breath, the weary going to and fro, the weary always
    knowing what comes next.

Fire

The boss, the crane operator, one of the workers, a friend of somebody
    in the junkyard—
whoever it is who watches me when I pull up to see the fire in the cab
    of the huge derrick,
the flames in crisp, hungry, emphatic shapes scaling the suddenly fragile-
    ribbed steel tower,
considers it a matter of deep, real suspicion that a stranger should bother
    to want to see this:
slouched against a stack of rusty, dismembered fenders, he regards me
    with a coolness bordering threat,
a wariness touching frank hostility, while, from a low warehouse building
    across the street,
another person, with a bulky fire extinguisher, comes, like someone from
    the UN, running,
red-faced, panting, with a look of anxious desperation, as though all the
    fault were his.

Fast Food

Musingly she mouths the end of her ballpoint pen as she stares down at
the sheet of paper.
A job application: lines, boxes, blanks to fill, a set of instructions, that
logo at the top.
Name and address, she's got that; phone number, age, high school, height
and weight: that.
Then number problems, addition, subtraction, a long, long division
. . . she hasn't got that.
It's blank next to that, the page is white next to that, her eyes touch down
on the white near that.
Never so white was white as that white: oh, white, angel of white, never
were you so pure,
never were you so seared by anyone's eyes and never so sadly bereft when
eyes lifted away,
when eyes left you and moved, indifferent and cool, across you to the
waiting door, oh, white, white.

The Orchid

with thanks to Curtis Ingham

"Tell me to touch your breast," I wanted to say: "Please, please, please
   touch my breast,"
I thought she wanted to say, but was too frightened, like me, too over-
   whelmed, too stricken,
like me, with the surges and furies of need; our lips, locked, ground
   together again and again,
we were bruised and swollen, like lovers in stories, sweating like lovers
   in bed, but no bed.
Then I heard, I thought, "Touch me," and ecstatic, I touched, but she
   brushed me away like a fly . . .
No, still held me, only my hand fell like a fly, her thirsty lips drank from
   me what they needed.
My testicles trembled, the orchid I'd paid five dollars for, hooked to the
   wires of her bra,
browned, faded, crumpled between us, as the orchid of memory crum-
   ples, mummified like a fly.

Work

Although constructed of the most up-to-date, technically advanced ele-
ments of woven glass,
carrying messages by laser pulse, the cable the telephone men are thread-
ing down the manhole
has exactly the same thickness and tense flexibility and has to be handled
with the same delicacy
as the penis of the huge palomino stallion I saw breeding at the riding
school when I was twelve
who couldn't get it in so that Charlie Young the little stablehand had to
help him with it.
How more than horrified I was that Charlie would touch the raw, un-
peeled, violet-purple thing,
thinking nothing of it, slipping between the flaring, snorting stud and
the gleaming mare,
lascivious and elegant, who, sidling under now, next year would throw
a mediocre foal, soon sold.

Peace

We fight for hours, through dinner, through the endless evening, who
    even knows now what about,
what could be so dire to have to suffer so for, stuck in one another's
    craws like fishbones,
the cadavers of our argument dissected, flayed, but we go on with it, to
    bed, and through the night,
feigning sleep, dreaming sleep, hardly sleeping, so precisely never touch-
    ing, back to back,
the blanket bridged across us for the wintry air to tunnel down, to keep
    us lifting, turning,
through the angry dark that holds us in its cup of pain, the aching dark,
    the weary dark,
then, toward dawn, I can't help it, though justice won't I know be served,
    I pull her to me,
and with such accurate, graceful deftness she rolls to me that we arrive
    embracing our entire lengths.

Men

As the garbage truck is backing up, one of the garbagemen is absorbed
    watching a pretty girl pass
and a sleeve of protruding steel catches him hard enough on the bicep
    to almost knock him down.
He clutches at his arm, limping heavily across the sidewalk, obviously
    in quite serious discomfort,
but the guy who works with him and who's seen the whole thing absolutely
    refuses to acknowledge
that his partner might be hurt, instead he bursts out laughing and starts
    making fun of the guy,
imitating the way he's holding himself, saying, "Booby-baby want a kiss?
    What's mattah, baby?"
Now the one who's hurt, grimacing, says, "Christ," shaking his head,
    vigorously rotating his arm.
Then, "You prick," he growls, and with a clunky leap and a great boom
    kicks the side of the truck.

Shame

A girl who, in 1971, when I was living by myself, painfully lonely, bereft, depressed,
offhandedly mentioned to me in a conversation with some friends that although at first she'd found me—
I can't remember the term, some dated colloquialism signifying odd, unacceptable, out-of-things—
she'd decided that I was after all all right . . . twelve years later she comes back to me from nowhere
and I realize that it wasn't my then irrepressible, unselective, incessant sexual want she meant,
which, when we'd been introduced, I'd naturally aimed at her and which she'd easily deflected,
but that she'd thought I really was, in myself, the way I looked and spoke and acted,
what she was saying, creepy, weird, whatever, and I am taken with a terrible humiliation.

On the Other Hand

On the other hand, in Philadelphia, long ago, at a party on Camac Street
    on a Sunday afternoon,
a springtime or an early autumn Sunday afternoon, I know, though the
    occasion's lost
and whose house it was is even lost, near the party's end, a girl, a woman,
    someone else's wife,
a beauty, too, a little older than I was, an "older woman," elegant and
    admirable and sober, too,
or nearly so, as I was coming down the stairs, put her hand on my hand
    on the landing,
caught me there and held me for a moment, with her hand, just her
    gentle hand, and with her look,
with how she looked at me, with some experience I didn't have, some
    delight I didn't understand,
and pulled me to her, hard, and kissed me, hard, to let me taste what
    subtle lusts awaited me.

Rungs

When we finally tracked him down, the old man (not really all that very
    old, we thought)
who'd made the comfortable, graceful, elegantly mortised chairs for all
    the farmers' kitchens
told us, never even opening the heavy iron gate into his yard, that he
    was through, retired,
done with it, and no, he didn't know anybody else who made them now,
    no one, he was the last.
He seemed to say it all with satisfaction, or at least was anyway unmoved
    by what it may have meant,
leaving us to back away, apologize, get into our car to make an awkward
    U-turn in his unpaved lane,
suffering meanwhile pangs of conscience and regret for honest good things
    gone for good,
all the innocence the world was losing, all the chances we'd once had,
    and lost, for beauty.

The Storm

A dense, low, irregular overcast is flowing rapidly in over the city from
    the middle South.
Above it, the sky holds blue, with scattered, intricate conglomerations of
    higher clouds
sidling in a much more even, stately procession across the dazzling,
    unsullied azure.
Now the lower level momentarily thins, fragments, and the early sun,
    still sharply angled,
breaks through into a finer veil and simmers, edges sharp, its ardent disk
    gently mottled.
Down across the roof lines, the decorative dome of Les Invalides looms,
    intruding on all this,
and suddenly a swallow banks around its gilded slopes, heading out but
    veering quickly back
as though the firmament, figured by so many volumes now, were too
    intimidating to row out in alone.

Blame

Where no question possibly remains—someone crying, someone dead
      —blame asks: whose fault?
It is the counterpart, the day-to-day, the real life, of those higher faculties
      we posit,
logic, reason, the inductions and deductions we yearningly trace the lines
      of with our finger.
It also has to do with nothing but itself, a tendency, a habit, like smoking
      or depression:
the unaccountable life quirks forecast in neither the soured milk nor the
      parents' roaring bed.
Relationship's theodicy: as the ever-generous deity leaves the difficult
      door of faith ajar
in a gesture of just-fathomable irony, so our beloved other, in the pain
      of partial mutuality,
moves us with its querulous "Look what you made me do!" towards the
      first clear glimpses of terrible self.

Medusa

Once, in Rotterdam, a whore once, in a bar, a sailors' bar, a hooker bar,
      opened up her legs—
her legs, my god, were logs—lifted up her skirt, and rubbed herself, with
      both hands rubbed herself,
there, right there, as though what was there was something else, as though
      the something else
was something she just happened to have under there, something that
      she wanted me to see.
All I was was twenty, I was looking for a girl, the girl, the way we always,
      all of us,
looked for the girl, and the woman leaned back there and with both
      hands she mauled it,
talked to it, asked it if it wanted me, laughed and asked me if I wanted
      it, while my virginity,
that dread I'd fought so hard to lose, stone by stone was rising back inside
      me like a wall.

Philadelphia: 1978

I'm on my way to the doctor to get the result of chest X-rays because I
    coughed blood
a few weeks ago while we were still in California; I am more or less a
    wreck of anxiety
and just as I turn the corner from Spruce Street onto Sixteenth where
    my doctor's is,
a raggedy-looking guy coming toward me on the sidewalk yells to me
    from fifty feet away:
"I know that walk! I sure know *that* walk!" smiling broadly, with genuine
    good feeling.
Although I don't recognize him—he looks druggy, wasted—I smile back,
    then, as we come closer,
he suddenly seems dubious, asking, "Don't I know you?" "Maybe not."
    "Weren't you in 'Nam?"
and before I can answer, "Shit!" he spits out, "shit!" furious with me:
    "You fucking *shit!*"

The Park

In that oblivious, concentrated, fiercely fetal decontraction peculiar to
    the lost,
a grimy derelict is flat out on a green bench by the sandbox, gazing
    blankly at the children.
"Do you want to play with me?" a small boy asks another, his fine head
    tilted deferentially,
but the other has a lovely fire truck so he doesn't have to answer and
    emphatically he doesn't,
he just grinds his toy, its wheels immobilized with grit, along the low
    stone wall.
The first child sinks forlornly down and lays his palms against the earth
    like Buddha.
The ankles of the derelict are scabbed and swollen, torn with aching
    varicose and cankers.
Who will come to us now? Who will solace us? Who will take us in
    their healing hands?

Travelers

He drives, she mostly sleeps; when she's awake, they quarrel, and now,
    in a violet dusk,
a rangy, raw-boned, efficient-looking mongrel loping toward them down
    the other shoulder
for no apparent reason swerves out on the roadbed just as a battered taxi
    is going by.
Horrible how it goes under, how it's jammed into the asphalt, compressed,
    abraded, crumpled,
then is ejected out behind, still, a miracle, alive, but spinning wildly on
    itself, tearing,
frenzied, at its broken spine, the mindless taxi never slowing, never
    noticing or caring,
they slowing, only for a moment, though, as, "Go on," she says, "go
    on, go on," face averted,
she can't look, while he, guilty as usual, fearful, fascinated and uncouth,
    can't not.

The Body

Jed says: How come I'm afraid to climb on the jungle game when even the littler kids aren't?

I say: But you did go up on it, I saw you before, you were going across the vine bridge.

Jed says: Yeah, I went up there, but I was afraid of the hard part, where you swing down.

I say: Well, people do things at different rates, there are things you can do that they can't.

Jed says: Am I a coward? Why couldn't I just swing right down there; I'm like the cowardly lion.

I say: When I was a kid I was just like you, I was always timid, I thought I was weak.

I say: I started doing sports late, like you, but look, now you're swimming and everything.

Jed says: I'm tired of swimming. What time is it? Can I get a crêpe? I don't think I'm weak.

Racists

Vas en Afrique! Back to Africa! the butcher we used to patronize in the
  Rue Cadet market,
beside himself, shrieked at a black man in an argument the rest of the
  import of which I missed
but that made me anyway for three years walk an extra street to a shop
  of definitely lower quality
until I convinced myself that probably I'd misunderstood that other thing
  and could come back.
Today another black man stopped, asking something that again I didn't
  catch, and the butcher,
who at the moment was unloading his rotisserie, slipping the chickens
  off their heavy spit,
as he answered—how get this right?—casually but accurately *brandished*
  the still-hot metal,
so the other, whatever he was there for, had subtly to lean away a little,
  so as not to flinch.

The Dream

How well I have repressed the dream of death I had after the war when
    I was nine in Newark.
It would be nineteen forty-six; my older best friend tells me what the
    atom bomb will do,
consume me from within, with fire, and that night, as I sat, bolt awake,
    in agony, it did:
I felt my stomach flare and flame, the edges of my heart curl up and
    char like burning paper.
All there was was waiting for the end, all there was was sadness, for in
    that awful dark,
that roar that never ebbed, that frenzied inward fire, I knew that everyone
    I loved was dead,
I knew that consciousness itself was dead, the universe shucked clean of
    mind as I was of my innards.
All the earth around me heaved and pulsed and sobbed; the orient and
    immortal air was ash.

Dawn

The first morning of mist after days of draining, unwavering heat along
    the shore: a *breath*:
a plume of sea fog actually visible, coherent, intact, with all of the quieter
    mysteries
of the sea implicit in its inconspicuous, unremarkable gathering in the
    weary branches
of the drought-battered spruce on its lonely knoll; it thins now, sidles
    through the browning needles,
is penetrated sharply by a sparrow swaying precipitously on a drop-
    glittering twiglet,
then another bird, unseen, is there, a singer, chattering, and another,
    long purls of warble,
which also from out of sight insinuate themselves into that dim, fragile,
    miniature cloud,
now, with almost visible reluctance, beginning its dissipation in the over-
    powering sunlight.

Reading: Winter

He's not sure how to get the jack on—he must have recently bought the
    car, although it's an ancient,
impossibly decrepit, barely holding-together Chevy: he has to figure out
    how each part works,
the base plate, the pillar, the thing that hooks to the bumper, even the
    four-armed wrench,
before he can get it all together, knock the hubcap off and wrestle free
    the partly rusted nuts.
This all happens on a bed of sheet ice: it's five below, the coldest January
    in a century.
Cars slip and skid a yard away from him, the flimsy jack is desperately,
    precariously balanced,
and meanwhile, when he goes into the trunk to get the spare, a page of
    old newspaper catches his attention
and he pauses, rubbing his hands together, shoulders hunched, for a full
    half minute, reading.

Reading: Early Sorrow

The father has given his year-old son *Le Monde* to play with in his stroller
and the baby does
just what you'd expect: grabs it, holds it out in front of him, stares
importantly at it,
makes emphatic and dramatic sounds of declamation, great pronounce-
ments of analytic probity,
then tears it, pulls a page in half, pulls the half in quarters, shoves a
hearty shred in his mouth—
a delicious editorial on unemployment and recession, a tasty *jeu de mots*
on government ineptitude.
He startles in amazement when the father takes the paper back from him:
What in heaven's name?
Indignation, impotence, frustration, outrage, petulance, rebellion, re-
alism, resignation.
Slumping back, disgusted . . . *Hypocrite lecteur, semblable* . . . Just wait,
he's muttering, just wait . . .

Suicide: Anne

for Anne Sexton

Perhaps it isn't as we like to think, the last resort, the end of something,
    thwarted choice or attempt,
but rather the ever-recurring beginning, the faithful first to mind, the
    very image of endeavor,
so that even the most patently meaningless difficulties, a badly started
    nail, a lost check,
not to speak of the great and irresolvable emotional issues, would bring
    instantly to mind
that unfailingly reliable image of a gesture to be carried out for once with
    confidence and grace.
It would feel less like desperation, being driven down, ground down, and
    much more a reflex, almost whim,
as though the pestering forces of inertia that for so long had held you
    back had ebbed at last,
and you could slip through now, not to peace particularly, not even to
    escape, but to completion.

Love: Youth

Except for the undeniable flash of envy I feel, the reflexive competitive-
  ness, he's inconsequential:
all I even see of him is the nape of his neck with his girlfriend's fingers
  locked in his hair.
She, though, looks disturbingly like a girl I wanted and pestered and who
  I thought broke my heart
when I was at that age of being all absorbed in just the unattainabilities
  she represented.
With what unashamed ardor this one is kissing, head working, that hand
  tugging him ever tighter,
and when at last they come apart, with what *gratitude* she peers at him,
  staring into his eyes
with what looks like nothing but relief, as though she'd waited her whole
  life for this, died for this,
time has taken so long for this, I thought you'd never get here, I thought
  I'd wither first and fade.

Love: Beginnings

They're at that stage where so much desire streams between them, so
    much frank need and want,
so much absorption in the other and the self and the self-admiring entity
    and unity they make—
her mouth so full, breast so lifted, head thrown back so far in her laughter
    at his laughter,
he so solid, planted, oaky, firm, so resonantly factual in the headiness
    of being craved so,
she almost wreathed upon him as they intertwine again, touch again,
    cheek, lip, shoulder, brow,
every glance moving toward the sexual, every glance away soaring back
    in flame into the sexual—
that just to watch them is to feel again that hitching in the groin, that
    filling of the heart,
the old, sore heart, the battered, foundered, faithful heart, snorting again,
    stamping in its stall.

Love: Wrath

He was very much the less attractive of the two: heavyset, part punk, part
    L. L. Bean,
both done ineptly; his look as brutal as the bully's who tormented you
    in second grade.
She was delicate and pretty; what she was suffering may have drawn her
    features finer.
As I went by, he'd just crossed his arms and said, "*You're* the one who's
    fucking us all up!"
He snarled it with a cruelty which made him look all the more a thug,
    and which astonished me,
that he would dare to speak to her like that, be so unafraid of losing her
    unlikely beauty . . .
But still, I knew, love, what he was feeling: the hungering for reason,
    for fair play,
the lust for justice; all the higher systems "Go": the need, the fear, the
    awe, burned away.

Good Mother: Out

"I want," he says again, through his tears, in this unfamiliar voice, again,
     "I want, I want,"
not even knowing why he says it now, says it yet again, only knowing
     that he has to say it,
even when she's told him calmly why he can't, then hissed the reasons
     why of course he can't,
then hit him, on the bottom, hard, again, again, and meaning it, so that
     he's crying, sobbing,
but though he sees her growing desperate, though he knows she'll hit
     him again, he says again,
"I want, I want, I want," though he really doesn't care now, doesn't even
     want what might be wanted:
why keep saying it? tears aflow, sobs like painful stones, why must he
     keep on with it?
Does he love her less? Is their relationship ever henceforth to be this?
     Desire, denial, despair?

Vehicle: Conscience

That moment when the high-wire walker suddenly begins to falter, wob-
ble, sway, arms flailing,
that breathtakingly rapid back-and-forth aligning-realigning of the dis-
placed center of gravity,
weight thrown this way, no, too far; that way, no, too far again, until
the movements themselves
of compensation have their rhythms established so that there's no way
possibly to stop now . . .
that very moment, wheeling back and forth, back and forth, appeal,
repeal, negation,
just before he lets it go and falls to deftly catch himself going by the wire,
somersaulting up,
except for us it never ceases, testing moments of the mind-weight this
way, back and back and forth,
no reestablishing of balance, no place to start again, just this, this force,
this gravity and fear.

Vehicle: Absence

The way, her father dead a day ago, the child goes in his closet, finds
      herself inside his closet,
finds herself atop the sprawl of emptied shoes, finds herself enveloped in
      the heavy emptied odor,
and breathes it in, that single, mingled gust of hair and sweat and father-
      flesh and father,
breathes it in and tries to hold it, in her body, in her breath, keep it in
      her breath forever . . .
so we, in love, in absence, in an absence so much less than death but
      still shaped by need and loss,
so we too find only what we want in sense, the drive toward sense, the
      hunger for the actual flesh;
so we, too, breathe in, as though to breathe was now itself the end of
      all, as though to scent,
to hold the fading traces of an actual flesh, was all, the hungering senses
      driven toward all . . .

Vehicle: Violence

The way boxers postulate a feeling to label that with which they overcome
      the body's vile fears,
its wish to flinch, to flee, break and run . . . they call it anger, pride,
      the primal passion to prevail;
the way, before they start, they glare at one another, try to turn themselves
      to snarling beasts . . .
so we first make up something in the soul we name and offer credence
      to—"meaning," "purpose," "end"—
and then we cast ourselves into the conflict, turn upon our souls, snarl
      like snarling beasts . . .
And the way the fighters fight, coolly until strength fails, then desperately,
      wildly, as in a dream,
and the way, done, they fall in one another's arms, almost sobbing with
      relief, sobbing with relief:
so we contend, so we wish to finish, wish to cry and end, but we never
      cry, never end, as in a dream.

Le Petit Salvié

for Paul Zweig

1935–1984

1

The summer has gone by both quickly and slowly. It's been a kind of eternity, each day
spinning out its endlessness, and yet with every look back, less time is left . . .

So quickly, and so slowly . . . In the tiny elevator of the flat you'd
      borrowed on the Rue de Pondicherry,
you suddenly put your head against my chest, I thought to show how
      tired you were, and lost consciousness,
sagging heavily against me, forehead oiled with sweat, eyes ghastly agape
      . . . so quickly, so slowly.
Quickly the ambulance arrives, mewling at the curb, the disinterested
      orderlies strap you to their stretcher.
Slowly at the clinic, waiting for the doctors, waiting for the ineffectual
      treatments to begin.
Slowly through that night, then quickly all the next day, your last day,
      though no one yet suspects it.
Quickly those remaining hours, quickly the inconsequential tasks and
      doings of any ordinary afternoon.
Quickly, slowly, those final silences and sittings I so regret now not having
      taken all of with you.

2

"I don't think we'll make the dance tonight," I mumble mawkishly. "It's
      definitely worse," you whisper.
Ice pack hugged to you, you're breathing fast; when you stop answering
      questions, your eyes close.
You're there, and then you slip away into your meditations, the way, it
      didn't matter where,

in an airport, a café, you could go away into yourself to work, and so
      we're strangely comforted.
It was dusk, late, the softening, sweetening, lingering light of the endless
      Paris evening.
Your room gave on a garden, a perfect breeze washed across your bed,
      it wasn't hard to leave you,
we knew we'd see you again: we kissed you, Vikki kissed you, "Goodbye,
      my friends," you said,
lifting your hand, smiling your old warming smile, then you went into
      your solitude again.

3

We didn't know how ill you were . . . we knew how ill but hid it . . .
      we didn't know how ill you were . . .
Those first days when your fever rose . . . if we'd only made you go into
      the hospital in Brive . . .
Perhaps you could have had another year . . . but the way you'd let death
      touch your life so little,
the way you'd learned to hold your own mortality before you like an
      unfamiliar, complex flower . . .
Your stoicism had become so much a part of your identity, your virtue,
      the system of your self-regard;
if we'd insisted now, you might have given in to us, when we didn't,
      weren't we cooperating
with what wasn't just your wish but your true passion never to be dying,
      sooner dead than dying?
You did it, too: composed a way from life directly into death, the ignoble
      scribblings between elided.

4

It must be some body-thing, some species-thing, the way it comes to take
      me from so far,
this grief that tears me so at moments when I least suspect it's there,
      wringing tears from me

I'm not prepared for, had no idea were even there in me, this most
    unmanly gush I almost welcome,
these cries so general yet with such power of their own I'm stunned to
    hear them come from me.
Walking through the street, I cry, talking later to a friend, I try not to
    but I cry again,
working at my desk I'm taken yet again, although, again, I don't want
    to be, not now, not again,
though that doesn't mean I'm ready yet to let you go . . . what it does
    mean I don't think I know,
nor why I'm so ill prepared for this insistence, this diligence with which
    consciousness afflicts us.

5

I imagine you rising to something like heaven: my friend who died last
    year is there to welcome you.
He would know the place by now, he would guide you past the ledges
    and the thorns and terror.
Like a child I am, thinking of you rising in the rosy clouds and being
    up there with him,
being with your guru Baba, too, the three of you, all strong men, all
    partly wild children,
wandering through my comforting child's heaven, doing what you're
    supposed to do up there forever.
I tell myself it's silly, all of this, absurd, what we sacrifice in attaining
    rational mind,
but there you are again, glowing, grinning down at me from somewhere
    in the heart of being,
ablaze with wonder and a child's relief that this after all is how astonish-
    ingly it finishes.

6

In my adult mind, I'm reeling, lost—I can't grasp anymore what I even
    think of death.

I don't know even what we hope for: ecstasy? bliss? or just release from
being, not to suffer anymore.
At the grave, the boring rabbi said that you were going to eternal rest:
rest? why rest?
Better say we'll be absorbed into the "Thou," better be consumed in
light, in Pascal's "Fire"!
Or be taken to the Godhead, to be given meaning now, at last, the
meaning we knew eluded us.
God, though, Godhead, Thou, even fire: all that is gone now, gone
the dark night arguments,
gone the partial answers, the very formulations fail; I grapple for the
questions as *they* fail.
Are we to be redeemed? When? How? After so much disbelief, will
something be beyond us to receive us?

7

Redemption is in life, "beyond" unnecessary: it is radically demeaning
to any possible divinity
to demand that life be solved by yet another life: we're compressed into
this single span of opportunity
for which our gratitude should categorically be presumed; this is what
eternity for us consists of,
praise projected from the soul, as love first floods outward to the other
then back into the self . . .
Yes, yes, I try to bring you to this, too; yes, what is over now is over;
yes, we offer thanks,
for what you had, for what we all have: this portion of eternity is no
different from eternity,
they both contract, expand, cast up illusion and delusion and all the
comfort that we have is love,
praise, the grace not to ask for other than we have . . . yes and yes, but
this without conviction, too.

8

What if after, though, there is something else, will there be judgment
      then, will it be retributive,
and if it is, if there is sin, will you have to suffer some hellish match
      with what your wrongs were?
So much good you did, your work, your many kindnesses, the befriend-
      ings and easy generosities.
What sort of evil do we dare imagine we'd have to take into those awful
      rectifications?
We hurt one another, all of us are helpless in that, with so much vul-
      nerable and mortal to defend.
But that vulnerability, those defenses, our belittling jealousies, resent-
      ments, thrusts and spites
are the very image of our frailty: shouldn't our forgiveness for them and
      our absolution be assumed?
Why would our ultimate identities be burdened with absolutes, imper-
      atives, lost discordant hymns?

9

How ambiguous the triumphs of our time, the releasing of the intellect
      from myth and magic.
We've gained much, we think, from having torn away corrupted modes
      of aggrandizement and giantism,
those infected and infecting errors that so long held sway and so bloated
      our complacencies
that we would willingly inflict even on our own flesh the crippling im-
      plications of our metaphysic.
How much we've had to pay, though, and how dearly had to suffer for
      our liberating dialectics.
The only field still left to us to situate our anguish and uncertainty is in
      the single heart,
and how it swells, the heart, to bear the cries with which we troubled
      the startled heavens.
Now we have the air, transparent, and the lucid psyche, and gazing
      inward, always inward, to the wound.

10

The best evidence I have of you isn't my memory of you, or your work,
 although I treasure both,
and not my love for you which has too much of me in it as subject, but
 the love others bore you,
bear you, especially Vikki, who lived out those last hard years with you,
 the despairs and fears,
the ambivalences and withdrawals, until that final week of fever that
 soaked both your pillows.
Such a moving irony that your last days finally should have seared the
 doubt from both of you.
Sometimes it's hard to tell exactly whom I cry for—you, that last night
 as we left you there,
the way you touched her with such solicitude, or her, the desolation she
 keeps coming to:
*"I've been facing death, touched death, and now I have a ghost I love
 and who loves me."*

11

Genevieve, your precious Gen, doesn't quite know when to cry, or how
 much she's supposed to cry,
or how to understand those moments when it passes, when she's distracted
 into play and laughter
by the other kids or by the adults who themselves don't seem to grasp
 this terrible non-game.
At the cemetery, I'm asked to speak to her, comfort her: never more
 impossible to move beyond cliché.
We both know we're helplessly embedded in ritual: you wanted her, I
 tell her, to be happy,
that's all, all her life, which she knows, of course, but nods to, as she
 knows what I don't say,
the simplest self-revealing truths, your most awful fear, the brutal fact of
 your mortality:
how horribly it hurt to go from her, how rending not being here to help
 bear this very pain.

12

Nothing better in the world than those days each year with you, your
      wife, my wife, the children,
at your old stone house in the Dordogne, looking over valleys one way,
      chestnut woods the other,
walks, long talks, visits to Lascaux or Les Eyzies, reading, listening to
      each other read.
Our last night, though, I strolled into the moonless fields, it might have
      been a thousand centuries ago,
and something suddenly was with me: just beyond the boundaries of my
      senses presences were threatening,
something out of childhood, mine or humankind's; I felt my fear, fa-
      miliar, unfamiliar, fierce,
might freeze me to the dark, but I looked back—I wasn't here alone,
      your house was there,
the zone of warmth it made was there, you yourself were there, circled
      in the waiting light.

13

I seem to have to make you dead, dead again, to hold you in my mind
      so I can clearly have you,
because unless I do, you aren't dead, you're only living somewhere out
      of sight, I'll find you,
soon enough, no need to hurry, and my mind slips into this other tense,
      other grammar of condition,
in which you're welded to banalities of fact and time, the reality of what
      is done eluding me.
If you're accessible to me, how can you be dead? You are accessible to
      me, therefore . . . something else.
So what I end with is the death of death, but not as it would have been
      elaborated once,
in urgencies of indignation, resignation, faith: I have you neither here,
      nor there, but not not-anywhere:
the soul keeps saying that you might be here, or there—the incessant
      passions of the possible.

14

Here's where we are: out behind the house in canvas chairs, you're reading
     new poems to me,
as you have so often, in your apartment, a park in Paris—anywhere:
     sidewalk, restaurant, museum.
You read musically, intensely, with flourishes, conviction: I might be
     the audience in a hall,
and you are unimaginably insecure, you so want me to admire every
     poem, every stanza, every line,
just as I want, need, you, too, to certify, approve, legitimize, all without
     a doubt or reservation,
and which neither of us does, improving everything instead, suggesting
     and correcting and revising,
as we knew, however difficult it was, we had to, in our barely overcome
     but overcome competitiveness.
How I'll miss it, that so tellingly accurate envy sublimated into warmth
     and brothership.

15

Here's where we are: clearing clumps of shrub and homely brush from
     the corner of your yard,
sawing down a storm-split plum tree, then hacking at the dozens of
     malevolently armored maguey:
their roots are frail as flesh and cut as easily, but in the August heat the
     work is draining.
Now you're resting, you're already weak although neither of us will admit
     it to the other.
Two weeks later, you'll be dead, three weeks later, three months, a year,
     I'll be doing this,
writing this, bound into this other labor that you loved so much and that
     we also shared,
still share, somehow always will share now as we shared that sunny late-
     summer afternoon,
children's voices, light; you, pale, leaning on the wall, me tearing at the
     vines and nettles.

16

"A man's life cannot be silent; living is speaking, dying, too, is speaking,"
    so you wrote,
so we would believe, but still, how understand what the finished life
    could have meant to say
about the dying and the death that never end, about potential gone,
    inspiration unaccomplished,
love left to narrow in the fallacies of recall, eroding down to partial gesture,
    partial act?
And we are lessened with it, amazed at how much our self-worth and
    joy were bound into the other.
There are no consolations, no illuminations, nothing of that long-awaited
    flowing toward transcendence.
There is, though, compensation, the simple certainty of having touched
    and having been touched.
The silence and the speaking come together, grief and gladness come
    together, the disparates fuse.

17

Where are we now? Nowhere, anywhere, the two of us, the four of us,
    fifty of us at a *fête*.
Islands of relationship, friends and friends, the sweet, normal, stolid
    matrix of the merely human,
the circles of community that intersect within us, hold us, touch us
    always with their presence,
even as, today, mourning, grief, themselves becoming memory, there
    still is that within us which endures,
not in possession of the single soul in solitude, but in the covenants of
    affection we embody,
the way an empty house embodies elemental presences, and the way,
    attentive, we can sense them.
Breath held, heart held, body stilled, we attend, and they are there,
    covenant, elemental presence,
and the voice, in the lightest footfall, the eternal wind, leaf and earth,
    the constant voice.

18

"The immortalities of the moment spin and expand; they seem to have
no limits, yet time passes.
These last days here are bizarrely compressed, busy, and yet full of
suppressed farewells . . ."
The hilly land you loved, lucerne and willow, the fields of butterfly and
wasp and flower.
Farewell the crumbling house, barely held together by your ministrations,
the shed, the pond.
Farewell your dumb French farmer's hat, your pads of yellow paper,
your joyful, headlong scrawl.
The coolness of the woods, the swallow's swoop and whistle, the confident
call of the owl at night.
Scents of dawn, the softening all-night fire, char, ash, warm embers in
the early morning chill.
The moment holds, you move across the path and go, the light lifts,
breaks: goodbye, my friend, farewell.

FROM

A Dream of Mind

[1 9 9 2]

When

As soon as the old man knew he was actually dying, even before anyone
    else would admit it,
he wanted out of the business, out of the miserable game, and he told
    whoever would listen,
whenever they'd listen, wife, family, friends, that he'd do it himself but
    how could he,
without someone to help, unable to walk as he was, get out of bed or
    up from the toilet himself?

At first he'd almost been funny: "Somebody comes, somebody goes,"
    he'd said on the birth of a niece,
and one day at lunch, "Please pass the cream cheese," then, deadpan,
    "That's all I'll miss."
But now he's obsessed: "Why won't you help me?" he says to his children,
    ten times a day,
a hundred and ten, but what if such meddling's wrong, and aren't these
    last days anyway precious?

Still, he was wearing them down: "This is no fun," he said to a son
    helping him hobble downstairs,
and the son, knowing full well what he meant, dreading to hear what
    he meant, had to ask, "What?"
so the old man, the biopsy incision still lumping the stubble of hair on
    the side of his skull,
could look in his eyes and say, if not as an accusation then nearly, "Death,
    dying: you know."

By then they knew, too, that sooner or later they'd have to give in, then
    sooner was over,
only later was looming, aphasiac, raving too late, so they held council
    and argued it out,
and though his daughter, holding onto lost hopes, was afraid, they decided
    to help him,

and told the old man, who said, "Finally, at last," and then to his
daughter, "Don't be afraid."

On the day it would happen, the old man would be funny again: wolfing
down handfuls of pills,
"I know this'll upset my stomach," he'd say, but for now he only asks
how it will happen.
"You'll just sleep," he's told, and "That's great" is his answer: "I haven't
slept for weeks."
Then "Great" again, then, serious, dry-eyed, to his weeping family: "Just
don't tell me when."

Allies: According to Herodotus

"Just how much are you worth?" Xerxes asks Pythius, reputedly the richest
    man in Lydia,
at the entertainment Pythius was holding in his palace for Xerxes and
    his chiefs of staff.
"Exactly three million nine hundred and ninety-three thousand golden
    darics," Pythius answers,
"and all of it is yours, my humble contribution towards your glorious
    war against the Greeks."

Xerxes is pleased: since he's left Persia with his troops, only Pythius along
    their route
has offered hospitality without being compelled to; all this might indicate
    a welcome drift.
"Consider yourself my personal friend," he says to Pythius: "Keep your
    fortune, you've earned it,
and furthermore I'm awarding you another seven thousand darics of my
    own to round it off."

Later, as Xerxes is preparing to go on, an eclipse is sighted, which ir-
    rationally alarms Pythius,
but also encourages him to ask Xerxes for a favor. "Anything you want
    just ask," says Xerxes.
"I have five sons," Pythius replies, "and all of them are leaving to take
    part in your campaign.
I'm getting on: let me keep my eldest here, to help take care of me and
    see to my estates."

Xerxes is incensed. "You ungrateful scum," he snarls, "you have the gall
    to talk about your son,
when I myself, Xerxes himself, is going off to fight with all my sons and
    friends and relatives?
It would have pleased my ears if you'd offered me your *wife*, and thrown
    in your old carcass.

195

You saved yourself by your generosity the other night, but now you'll
       know a real king's rage."

Some ancients doubt Herodotus, but not in this; Xerxes, after all, angry
       at the Hellespont,
had it lashed and branded; we can trust therefore that near the moment
       when history begins,
Xerxes commanded that the beloved elder son of Pythius be brought to
       him and cut in half,
and that the halves be placed along the roadside for his army to march
       out towards Greece between.

Harm

With his shopping cart, his bags of booty and his wine, I'd always found
    him inoffensive.
Every neighborhood has one or two these days; ours never rants at you
    at least or begs.

He just forages the trash all day, drinks and sings and shadowboxes, then
    at nightfall
finds a doorway to make camp, set out his battered little radio and slab
    of rotting foam.

The other day, though, as I was going by, he stepped abruptly out between
    parked cars,
undid his pants, and, not even bothering to squat, sputtered out a noxious,
    almost liquid stream.

There was that, and that his bony shanks and buttocks were already stained
    beyond redemption,
that his scarlet testicles were blown up bigger than a bull's with some
    sorrowful disease,

and that a slender adolescent girl from down the block happened by right
    then, and looked,
and looked away, and looked at me, and looked away again, and made
    me want to say to her,

because I imagined what she must have felt, It's not like this, really, it's
    not this,
but she was gone, so I could think, But isn't it like this, isn't this just
    what it is?

The Insult

Even here, in a forest in the foothills of a range of mountains, lucent
air, the purest dawn,
a continent and years away from where it happened, it comes back to
me, simmering and stinging,
driving me farther down along the pathway to a hidden brook I hadn't
realized was there.

The thrust came first, accurate, deft, to the quick, its impetus and rea-
sonings never grasped.
Then my pain, my sullen, shocked retort, harsh, but with nothing like
an equivalent rancor.
Then the subsiding: nothing resolved, only let slide; nothing forgiven,
only put by.

The stream bends here under a bridge, its voice lifts more loudly from
the rocks of its bed.
The quickly hardening light slants in over the tough, sparse wild grasses
on the far hill.
Wind rattling the aspens; a hawk so tiny it seems almost a toy hovering
in a socket of updraft.

Even now, I have no real wish to tell it, I know it so well why have to
recite it again?
What keeps bringing us back to those fissures so tenaciously holding our
furious suffering?
Are there deeper wounds in us than we know; might grief itself be com-
munion and solace?

So many footprints crossing and recrossing the trail through the boulders
edging the bank;
the swarms of apparently purposeless insects ticking their angular circuits
over the water.
The song of the water, the mindless air, the hawk beyond sight, the
inaudible cry of its prey.

Child Psychology

for Loren Crabtree and Barbara Cram

In that stage of psychosexual development called latency, when not that
much, at least supposedly,
is going on—libido sleeps, the engrossing Oedipal adventure is forgotten
for a time—
we were going somewhere and without telling him I took my father's
keys and went outside to wait.
House, car, office keys: how proud I was to be the keeper of that weighty,
consequential mass.
I stood there, tossing it from hand to hand, then, like my father, high
into the air.
And then I missed, and saw it fall, onto the narrow grating of a storm
sewer, and then in.

I gazed, aghast, down into those viscous, unforgiving depths, intestinal,
malignant, menacing.
What happened? Had I dropped the keys on purpose? God no: I well
knew my father's hand.
They'd just fallen, by themselves, that's what I'd say; no, say nothing,
that was even better,
keep still, lips sealed, stoicism, silence—what other mechanism did I
have besides denial?
Which is what I implemented when my father came to question me,
and question me again.
Wholly taken in the burning ardor of my virtue, I was as innocent as
Isaac, and as dumb.

Months pass, the doorbell rings, as always I'm the one to run to answer;
a man is there,
he holds the long-forgotten ring of keys, my father's name, address, and
number legible, intact.
I don't remember what men wore back then to muck about in filth for
us, but it didn't matter;
the second I saw him I knew him—*the return of the repressed* . . . so
soon, though, so very soon.

199

The shudderings I drove within were deafening; I couldn't bring myself
    to speak, but knew he would,
as I knew what he would say: "Is your father home?" He was, he was:
    how could he not be?

Scar

As though the skin had been stripped and pulled back onto the skull like
 a stocking and soldered
too tightly so that it mottled to yellow and ocher, the pores and follicles
 thumbed out of the clay
by the furious slash of flame that must have leapt on her and by the
 healing that hurt her—

if it is healing that leaves her, age three, in a lassitude lax on her mother's
 broad lap,
bleak, weary, becalmed, what's left of her chin leaned heavily onto what's
 left of her fingers,
those knobs without nails, diminished, blunted, as though someone had
 hammered them thicker;

nares gone, ears gone, most of the dear lips gone so that your gaze is
 taken too deeply, terribly,
into the pool of the mouth as into a genital; the eyelids upper and lower
 wrinkled like linen,
the blood rims of the eyes too graphically vivid; harsh, tearless, porno-
 graphically red—

and you are supposed not to look or look and glance quickly away and
 not look at the mother,
who signs with a stone shoulder and eyes fixed to the child's white-gauze
 surgical cap
that if you do look you are cursed, if you do look you will and you well
 know it be damned.

Lascivious pity, luxurious pity, that glances and looks and looks twice
 and delivers the tear
and hauls out of the blind, locked caves of the breast these silent strangles
 of sobs
that ache but give something like tremulous whispers of sanctity back,
 psalms of gratification.

Lascivious pity, idle, despicable pity, pity of the reflexive half-thought
     holy thought
thinking the mindless threnody of itself once again: I watched, I couldn't
     not watch her,
as she so conscientiously, carefully wouldn't watch me; rapacious, pil-
     laging pity: forgive me.

FROM *Some of the Forms of Jealousy*

Signs

My friend's wife has a lover; I come to this conclusion—not suspicion,
    mind, conclusion,
not a doubt about it, not a hesitation, although how I get there might
    be hard to track;
a blink a little out of phase, say, with its sentence, perhaps a word or
    two too few;
a certain tenderness of atmosphere, of aura, almost like a pregnancy,
    with less glow, perhaps,
but similar complex inward blushes of accomplishment, achievement,
    pride—during dinner,
as she passes me a dish of something, as I fork a morsel of it off, as our
    glances touch.

My friend's manner, or his guise, is openness, heartiness and healthy
    haleness in all things;
the virtue of conviction, present moment, that sort of thing: it is his
    passion and his ethic,
so I don't know now if he knows or doesn't know, or knows and might
    be hiding it, or doesn't care.
He is hearty, open, present; he is eating dinner in the moment with his
    wife and old dear friend.
The wife, wifely, as she pours my wine and hands it to me looks across
    the glass's rim at me.
Something in the wifely glance tells me now she knows I know, and
    when I shyly look away,
reach across for bread and butter, she looks down at my hand, and up
    again: she is telling me
she doesn't care the least bit if I know or don't know, she might in fact
    wish me to know.

My friend is in the present still, taking sustenance; it's sustaining, good;
    he smiles, good.
Down below, I can just make out the engines of his ship, the stresses,
    creaks, and groans;

everything's in hand; I hear the happy workers at their chugging furnaces
and boilers.
I let my friend's guise now be not my guise but truth; in truth, I'm like
him, dense, convinced,
involved all in the moment, hearty, filled, fulfilled, not just with manner,
but with fact.
I ply my boilers, too; my workers hum: light the deck lamps, let the string
quartet play.

My friend's wife smiles and offers me her profile now; she is telling me
again: but why?
She smiles again, she glows, she plays me like a wind chime; I sit here
clanging to myself.
My friend doesn't seem to see me resonating; he grins, I grin, too, I flee
to him again.
I'm with him in his moment now, I'm in my mouth just as he's in his,
munching, hungrily, heartily.
My safe and sane and hungry mouth hefts the morsels of my sustenance
across its firmament.
The wife smiles yet again, I smile, too, but what I'm saying is if what
she means is so,
I have no wish to know; more, I never did know; more, if by any chance
I might have known,
I've forgotten, absolutely, yes: if it ever did come into my mind it's slipped
my mind.
In truth, I don't remember anything; I eat, I drink, I smile; I hardly even
know I'm there.

The Cautionary

A man who's married an attractive, somewhat younger woman conceives
    a painful jealousy of her.
At first he's puzzled as to why he should brood so fretfully on her faith-
    fulness or lack of it.
Their lovemaking is fulfilling: he enjoys it, his wife seems to, too, as
    much as he does,
or, to his surprise (he's never had this experience before), maybe more
    than he does.
When they married, it had seemed a miracle, he'd hardly been able to
    believe his great luck:
the ease and grace with which she'd come to him, the frank, good-
    humored way she'd touch him.
But now . . . it isn't that she gives too much meaning to sex, or exhibits
    insufficient affection,
it's how *involved* in it she gets, so nearly oblivious, in a way he can never
    imagine being.
He finds that he's begun to observe their life in bed with what he thinks
    is a degree of detachment.
He sees himself, his blemishes, the paunch he can't always hide, then
    her, her sheen, her glow.
Why, he asks, would such a desirable woman have committed herself
    so entirely to such as him?
And, more to the point: why this much passion, these urgencies and
    wants, this blind delight?
By a train of logic he can't trace to its source but which he finds chillingly
    irrefutable,
he decides that it's not he himself, as himself, his wife desires, but that
    she simply *desires*.
He comes to think he's incidental to this desire, which is general, un-
    specific, without object,
almost, in its intensity and heat, without a subject: she herself seems
    secondary to it,
as though the real project of her throaty, heaving passion was to melt
    her mindlessly away.

Why would such need be limited to him: wouldn't it sweep like a search-
   light across all maleness?
He can't help himself, he begins to put to the proof his disturbing but
   compelling observations.
When they're out together, it's self-evident to him that every man who
   sees her wants her:
all the furtive glances, behind, aside, even into surfaces that hold her
   image as she passes.
It dawns on him in a shocking and oddly exciting insight that for so many
   to desire her
some *signal* would have to be sent, not an actual gesture perhaps, nothing
   so coarse as a beckoning,
but something like an aura, of eagerness, availability, which she'd be
   subconsciously emitting.
Hardly noticing, he falls a step behind her, the better to watch her, to
   keep track of her.
Then he realizes to his chagrin that his scrutiny might very well be
   working on his wife.
In a sadly self-fulfilling prophecy, she might begin to feel vulnerable,
   irritated, disconnected;
yes, alone, she must often feel alone, as though he, wretch that he is,
   wasn't even there.
This is the last way he'd have thought that his obsession would undo
   him, but why not?
A woman among admiring men is already in the broadest sense a potential
   object of desire,
but a woman with a sharply heightened awareness of her most elementary
   sexual identity,
as his wife by now would have, with this jackal, as he now sees himself,
   sniffing behind her:
wouldn't she, even against her best intentions, manifest this in a primitive,
   perceptible way,
and wouldn't men have to be aware, however vaguely, that some sexual
   event was taking place?
Mightn't the glances she'd inspire reflect this, bringing an intriguing new
   sense of herself,
and mightn't this make even more likely that she'd betray him in just
   the way that he suspects?

Yes. No. Yes. He knows that he should stop all this: but how can he,
     without going to the end?
The end might be just the thing he's driving them both towards, he can't
     help himself, though,
he'll dissemble his fixations, but if there's to be relief, it will have to wait
     till then.

The Question

The middle of the night, she's wide awake, carefully lying as far away as
she can from him.
He turns in his sleep and she can sense him realizing she's not in the
place she usually is,
then his sleep begins to change, he pulls himself closer, his arm comes
comfortably around her.
"Are you awake?" she says, then, afraid that he might think she's asking
him for sex,
she hurries on, "I want to know something; last summer, in Cleveland,
did you have someone else?"
She'd almost said—she was going to say—"Did you have a *lover?*" but
she'd caught herself;
she'd been frightened by the word, she realized; it was much too definite,
at least for now.
Even so, it's only after pausing that he answers, "No," with what feeling
she can't tell.
He moves his hand on her, then with a smile in his voice asks, "Did
you have somebody in Cleveland?"
"That's not what I was asking you," she says crossly. "But that's what I
asked *you,*" he answers.
She's supposed to be content now, the old story, she knows that she's
supposed to be relieved,
but she's not relieved, her tension hasn't eased the slightest bit, which
doesn't surprise her.
She's so confused that she can't really even say now if she wants to believe
him or not.
Anyway, what about that pause? Was it because in the middle of the
night and six months later
he wouldn't have even known what she was talking about, or was it
because he needed that moment
to frame an answer which would neutralize what might after all have
been a shocking thrust
with a reasonable deflection, in this case, his humor: a laugh that's like
a lie and is.

"When would I have found the time?" he might have said, or, "Who in Cleveland could I love?"

Or, in that so brief instant, might he have been finding a way to stay in the realm of truth,

as she knew he'd surely want to, given how self-righteously he esteemed his ethical integrities?

It comes to her with a start that what she most deeply and painfully suspects him of is a *renunciation*.

She knows that he has no one now; she thinks she knows there's been no contact from Cleveland,

but she still believes that there'd been something then, and if it was as important as she thinks,

it wouldn't be so easily forgotten, it would still be with him somewhere as a sad regret,

perhaps a precious memory, but with that word, renunciation, hooked to it like a price tag.

Maybe that was what so rankled her, that she might have been the object of his charity, his *goodness*.

That would be too much; that he would have wronged her, then sacrificed himself for her.

Yes, "Lover," she should have said it, "Lover, lover," should have made him try to disavow it.

She listens to his breathing; he's asleep again, or has he taught himself to feign that, too?

"No, last summer in Cleveland I didn't have a lover, I have never been to Cleveland, I love you.

There is no Cleveland, I adore you, and, as you'll remember, there was no last summer:

the world last summer didn't yet exist, last summer still was universal darkness, chaos, pain."

Politics

They're discussing the political situation they've been watching evolve
    in a faraway country.
He's debating intensely, almost lecturing, about fanaticism and religion,
    the betrayal of ideals.
He believes he's right, but even as he speaks he knows within himself
    that it's all incidental;
he doesn't really care that much, he just can't help himself, what he's
    really talking about
is the attraction that he feels she feels towards those dark and passionate
    young men
just now glowing on the screen with all the unimpeachable righteousness
    of the once-oppressed.
He says that just because they've been afflicted isn't proof against their
    lying and conniving.
What he means is that they're not, because she might find them virile,
    therefore virtuous.
He says that there are always forces we don't see that use these things for
    evil ends.
What he means is that he's afraid that she might turn from him towards
    someone suffering,
or, as possible, towards someone who'd share with similar conviction her
    abhorrence of suffering.
He means he's troubled by how *sure* she is, how her compassions are so
    woven into her identity.
Isn't the degree to which she's certain of her politics, hence of her rightness
    in the world,
the same degree to which she'd be potentially willing to risk herself, and
    him, and everything?
Also, should she wish to justify an action in her so firmly grounded socio-
    ethical system,
any action, concupiscence, promiscuity, orgy, wouldn't it not only let
    her but abet her?
Sometimes he feels her dialectics and her assurance are assertions of some
    ultimate availability.

Does he really want someone so self-sufficient, who knows herself so
    well, knows so much?
In some ways, he thinks—has he really come to this?—he might want
    her knowing *nothing*.
No, not nothing, just . . . a little less . . . and with less fervor, greater
    pragmatism, realism.
More and more in love with her, touched by her, he still goes on, to his
    amazement, arguing.

Ethics

The only time, I swear, I ever fell more than abstractly in love with
      someone else's wife,
I managed to maintain the clearest sense of innocence, even after the
      woman returned my love,
even after she'd left her husband and come down on the plane from
      Montreal to be with me,
I still felt I'd done nothing immoral, that whole disturbing category had
      somehow been effaced;
even after she'd arrived and we'd gone home and gone to bed, and even
      after, the next morning,
when she crossed my room undressed—I almost looked away; we were
      both as shy as adolescents—
and all that next day when we walked, made love again, then slept,
      clinging to each other,
even then, her sleeping hand softly on my chest, her gentle breath gently
      moving on my cheek,
even then, or not until then, not until the new day touched upon us,
      and I knew, knew absolutely,
that though we might love each other, something in her had to have the
      husband, too,
and though she'd tried, and would keep trying to overcome herself, I
      couldn't wait for her,
did that perfect guiltlessness, that sure conviction of my inviolable virtue,
      flee me,
to leave me with a blade of loathing for myself, a disgust with who I
      guessed by now I was,
but even then, when I took her to the airport and she started up that
      corridor the other way,
and we waved, just waved—anybody watching would have thought that
      we were separating friends—
even then, one part of my identity kept claiming its integrity, its non-
      involvement, even chastity,

which is what I castigate myself again for now, not the husband or his
    pain, which he survived,
nor the wife's temptation, but the thrill of evil that I'd felt, then kept
    myself from feeling.

The Mirror

The way these days she dresses with more attention to go out to pass the
      afternoon alone,
shopping or just taking walks, she says, than when they go together to a
      restaurant or party:
it's such a subtle thing, how even speak of it, how imagine he'd be able
      to explain it to her?
The way she looks for such long moments in the mirror as she gets ready,
      putting on her makeup;
the way she looks so deeply at herself, gazes at her eyes, her mouth,
      down along her breasts:
what is he to say, that she's looking at herself in ways he's never seen
      before, more *carnally*?
She would tell him he was mad, or say something else he doesn't want
      no matter what to hear.
The way she puts her jacket on with a flourish, the way she gaily smiles
      going out the door,
the door, the way the door slams shut, the way its latch clicks shut behind
      her so emphatically.
What is he to think? What is he to say, to whom? The mirror, jacket,
      latch, the awful door?
He can't touch the door, he's afraid he'll break the frightening covenant
      he's made with it.
He can't look into the mirror, either, that dark, malicious void: who
      knows what he might see?

The Call

When one of my oldest and dearest friends died and another friend called
    to console me,
I found myself crying—I hadn't thought I would—and said, "I didn't
    know I'd feel this badly."
Now, a year later, the second friend calls again, this time because his
    mistress has left him.
He's anguished, his voice torn; "I didn't know," he tells me, "that I'd
    feel this badly."
I'm shocked to hear him use precisely the words I had in my grief, but
    of course I understand.
There are more calls, and more, but in the end they all add up to much
    the same thing.
The mistress had warned him time and again, if not in so many words,
    that this might happen;
she'd asked him to leave his wife, he hadn't yet, but thought his honest
    oath to was in effect.
How was he to know that what he'd taken as playful after-intercourse
    endearments were threats?
Now that this terrible thing has happened, he's promised he'll really do
    it, but too late:
his beloved has found someone else, she's in love, no question now of
    beginning over.
At first my friend's desperation is sad to behold, his self-esteem is in
    harrowing decline;
decisiveness, or a lack of it, his lack of it, has become the key factor in
    his value system.
Gradually, though, he begins to focus on the new lover, on his insip-
    idness, his pitiful accomplishments.
There are flaws to this attack, though, because with each new proof of
    the other's shortcomings,
with each attempt to neutralize his effectiveness, my friend's self-blame
    becomes more acute.
Still, he can't say to himself, "Behold this giant competitor, this (Freud-
    ian) father of a man,"

so he keeps diminishing the other, which only augments his sense of the capriciousness of fate.

Then, to his relief (though he won't quite admit it), he finds sometimes he's furious at the woman.

How could she have done this? She'd known the risks he'd taken in doubling his affections,

shouldn't she simply have accepted his ambivalence and hesitation as a part of their relation?

And what about his wife; yes, some innocence, some purity has been transgressed there, too.

Her suspicions had been hot; she'd accepted his denials; wasn't that an offering to the mistress?

Aren't there violations, then, not just of his own good intentions but of his wife's generosity?

He's often hot with rage now, he doesn't even know at whom, but then he has to stop himself.

He doesn't want to blame the mistress *too* much, in case she should, despite all, come back,

and he doesn't want to hate his wife, who still doesn't know, or is even kinder than he thought.

So he keeps dutifully forgiving everyone, which throws the whole fault back on him again

and makes him wonder what kind of realignment could possibly redeem so much despair?

No, it's all ruined in advance, everything is stuck, the only thing he can do now is forget.

They're so degrading, these issues which can be resolved by neither consolation nor forgiveness.

No wonder my friend would cast his misery as mourning; no wonder, biting my tongue, I'd let him.

The Image

She began to think that jealousy was only an excuse, a front, for something
      even more rapacious,
more maniacally pathological in its readiness to sacrifice its own well-
      being for its satisfaction.
Jealousy was supposed to be a fact of love, she thought, but this was a
      compulsion, madness,
it didn't have a thing to do with love, it was perfectly autonomous, love
      was just its vehicle.
She thought: wasn't there a crazy hunger, even a delight, in how he'd
      pounced on her betrayal?
There hadn't even *been* betrayal until he'd made it so; for her, before
      that, it had been a whim,
a frivolity she'd gone to for diversion, it hadn't had anything to do with
      him, or them.
Her apologies meant nothing, though, nor her fervent promise of re-
      pentance, he *held* his hurt,
he cultivated, stroked it, as though that was all that kept him in rela-
      tionship with her.
He wanted her to think she'd maimed him: what was driving him to such
      barbarous vindictiveness?
She brought to mind a parasite, waiting half a lifetime for its victim to
      pass beneath its branch,
then coming to fully sentient, throbbing, famished life and without hes-
      itation letting go.
It must have almost starved in him, she thinks, all those years spent
      scenting out false stimuli,
all that passive vigilance, secreting bitter enzymes of suspicion, ingesting
      its own flesh;
he must have eaten at himself, devouring his own soul until his chance
      had finally come.
But now it had and he had driven fangs in her and nothing could contain
      his terrible tenacity.
She let the vision take her further; they had perished, both of them, there
      they lay, decomposing,

one of them drained white, the other bloated, gorged, stale blood oozing
through its carapace.

Only as a stupid little joke, she thought, would anybody watching dare
wonder which was which.

The Silence

He hasn't taken his eyes off you since we walked in, although you seem
    not to notice particularly.
Only sometimes, when your gaze crosses his, mightn't it leave a very
    tiny *tuft* behind?
It's my imagination surely, but mightn't you be all but imperceptibly
    acknowledging his admiration?
We've all known these things; the other, whom we've never seen before,
    but whose ways we recognize,
and with whom we enter into brilliant complicities; soul's receptors tuned
    and armed;
the concealed messages, the plots, the tactics so elegant they might have
    been rehearsed:
the way we wholly disregard each other, never, except at the most casually
    random intervals,
let our scrutinies engage, but then that deep, delicious draft, that eager
    passionate appreciation . . .
I tell myself that I don't care, as I might not sometimes, when no rival's
    happened by,
but I do care now, I care acutely, I just wonder what the good would be
    if I told you I can see
your mild glances palpably, if still so subtly, furtively, intertwining now
    with his?
I'd only be insulting you, violating my supposed trust in you, belittling
    both of us.
We've spent so much effort all these years learning to care for one
    another's sensitivities.
In an instant that's all threatened; your affections seem as tenuous as
    when we met,
and I have to ask myself, are you more valuable to me the more that
    you're at risk?
Am I to you? It's degrading, thinking we're more firmly held together by
    our mutual anxiety.
If my desire is susceptible to someone else's valuations of its object, then
    what am I?

Can I say that my emotions are my own if in my most intimate affection
such contaminations lurk?

Still, though, what if this time I'd guessed right, and what if I should try
to tell you,

to try to laugh about it with you, to use our union, and our hard-earned
etiquettes to mock him,

this intruder—look—who with his dream of even daring to attempt you
would be ludicrous?

There would still be risks I almost can't let myself consider: that you'd
be humoring me,

that the fierce intensity of your attraction to him would already constitute
a union with him,

I'd be asking you to lie and doing so you'd be thrown more emphatically
into his conspiracy;

your conniving with him would relegate me to the status of an obligation,
a teary inconvenience.

This is so exhausting: when will it relent? It seems never, not as long as
consciousness exists.

Therefore, as all along I knew I would, as I knew I'd have to, I keep still,
conceal my sorrow.

Therefore, when you ask, "Is something wrong?" what is there to answer
but, "Of course not, why?"

Soliloquies

1

Strange that sexual jealousy should be so much like sex itself: the same
    engrossing reveries,
the intricate, voluptuous pre-imaginings, the impatient plottings towards
    a climax, then climax . . .
Or, not quite climax, since jealousy is different in how uninvolved it is
    in consummation.
What is its consummation but negation? Not climax but relief, a sigh of
    resignation, disappointment.
Still, how both depend upon a judicious intermingling of the imaginary
    and the merely real,
and how important image is for both, the vivid, breath-held unscrolling
    of fugitive inner effigies.
Next to all our other minds, how pure both are, what avid concentration
    takes us in them.
Maybe this is where jealousy's terrific agitation comes from, because, in
    its scalding focus,
a desperate single-mindedness is imposed upon the soul and the sad,
    conditioned soul responds,
so fervently, in such good faith, it hardly needs the other person for its
    delicious fever.
Is there anything in life in which what is fancied is so much more intense
    than what's accomplished?
We know it's shadow, but licentious consciousness goes on forever man-
    ufacturing . . . fever.

2

The stupidity of it, the repetitiveness, the sense of all one's mental mech-
    anisms run amok.
Knowing that pragmatically, statistically, one's fantasies are foolish, but
    still being trapped.

221

The almost unmanageable foreboding that one's character won't be up
    to its own exigencies.
Knowing one is one's own victim; how self-diminishing to have to ask,
    "Who really *am* I, then?"
I am someone to be rescued from my mind, but the agent of my suffering
    is its sole redemption;
only someone else, a specific someone else, can stop me from inflicting
    this upon myself.
And so within myself, in this unsavory, unsilent solitude of self, I fall
    into an odious dependency.
I'm like an invalid relying absolutely on another's rectitude; but the
    desperate invalid, abandoned,
would have at least the moral compensation of knowing that he wasn't
    doing this to himself;
philosophically, his reliance would be limited by the other's sense of
    obligation, or its absence.
This excruciating, groundless need becomes more urgent, more to be
    desired the more it's threatened,
while its denouement promises what one still believes will be an un-
    imaginably luxurious release.

3

I try to imagine the kind of feeling which would come upon me if I really
    were betrayed now.
How long would I remain in that abject state of mind? When would it
    end? Am I sure it would?
What constitutes a state of mind at all? Certain chunks of feeling, of
    pleasure or pain?
I postulate the pain, but can I really? My mood prevents it. Is that all I
    am, then, mood?
Sometimes I feel firmly socketed within myself; other moments, I seem
    barely present.
Which should I desire? Mightn't it be better not to feel anything if I'm
    helpless anyway?
I try to reconceive the problem: I am he who will forgive his being
    wronged, but can I know I will?

All my mind will tell me absolutely and obsessively is that its future isn't
     in my governance.
Might that be why the other's possible offense seems much more *rank*
     than mine would ever be?
My betrayal would be whimsical, benign, the hymen of my innocence
     would be quickly reaffirmed.
Hers infects, contaminates, is ever the first premeditated step of some
     squalid longer term.
I would forgive, but suspect that she might already be beyond forgiveness:
     whose fault then?

4

What would be the difference? The way jealousy seeps into my notions
     of intention and volition,
the annihilating force it has: mightn't it be grounded in the furies of more
     radical uncertainty?
That nothing lasts, that there's no real reason why it doesn't last, and
     that there's death,
and more maddening still that existence has conjectured possibilities of
     an after-death,
but not their certainty, rather more the evidence that any endlessness is
     mental fiction.
And that there might be a God, a potentially beloved other who *would*
     know, this, and everything,
who already has sufficient knowledge of our fate to heal us but may well
     decide not to do so.
How not rage, how, in love, with its promises of permanence, the only
     answer to these doubts,
not find absurd that this, too, should suffer from foreboding, and one so
     mechanically averted?
Might jealousy finally suggest that what we're living isn't ever what we
     think we are?
What, though, would more require our love, our being loved, our vow
     of faithfulness and faith?
And what would more compel that apprehensive affirmation: *I'll love you
     forever, will you me?*

FROM *A Dream of Mind*

Shadows

They drift unobtrusively into the dream, they linger, then they depart,
          but they emanate, always,
an essence of themselves, an aura, of just the frequency my mind needs
          to grasp and contain them.
Sometimes, though, the identity that I sense there, the person I feel
          intimated or implied,
is so fluid and changes so rapidly and dramatically that often I hardly
          know who I'm with.
Someone is there, then they're someone from another moment of my
          life, or even a stranger.
At first I find such volatile mutability surprisingly less agitating than I'd
          have thought,
probably because these others brought and taken away by the dream
          manifest such careless unconcern.
Before long, though, I feel apprehensive: I find that whenever someone
          in the dream changes,
I subtly alter who I am as well, so as to stay in a proper relation with
          this new arrival
who may already be somebody else, someone for whom the self I've come
          up with is obsolete.
Suddenly I'm never quite who I should be; beset by all this tenuous
          veering and blurring,
my character has become the function of its own revisïons; I'm a bystander
          in my own dream.
Even my response to such flux is growing unstable; until now I've con-
          sidered it speculatively,
but what says I'm not going to stay in this epistemologically tremulous
          state forever?
I find I'm trying to think how to stop this, but trying to think in dream
          means, as always,
trying to *do*, and what do now with this presence moving towards me,
          wavering, shifting,
now being itself, now another, webbed now in the shadows of memory,
          now brilliant, burning?

Am I to try to engage it, or turn back to myself to steel myself in a more
    pure concentration?
Even as I watch, it transfigures again; I see it, if it is it, as through ice,
    or a lens.
I feel a breath touch me now, but is it this breath I feel or someone's I
    haven't met yet,
is it a whisper I hear or the murmur of multitudes sensing each other
    closer within me?
How even tell who I am now, how know if I'll ever be more than the
    field of these interchangings?

The Solid

Although I'm apparently alone, with a pleasant but unextraordinary feel-
ing of self-sufficiency,
I know I'm actually a part of a group of people who for reasons the dream
never makes clear
are unavailable to any of my senses, though I'm always aware of the
pressure of their presence.
No matter what else I'm doing, no matter how scant the attention I pay,
I know they're there,
only my response to being in relation with beings I can only imagine
alters now and again.
Usually I'm comforted: this intuition seems to impart to the dream such
stability as it has.
Immersed with my mysterious companions in an enormous, benign,
somehow consoling solid,
all that's required is that I not carelessly set jolts out into that sensitive
bulk of otherness.
At other, nearly simultaneous moments, I feel signals sent, intentionally
or not, I can't tell,
which arrive to my consciousness as an irritation, almost an abrasion of
the material of thought.
In some far corner of dream, someone wants, needs, with such vehement,
unreasonable fervor,
that even from here I'm afflicted with what I can only believe is an
equivalent chagrin.
I try to think of ways to send back if not reassurance then an acknowl-
edgment of my concern,
but I realize this would require not only energy and determination but
a discernment, a delicacy,
the mere thought of which intimidates me, reinforcing the sense I have
of my ineffectiveness.
I begin to be afraid then, the dream is deteriorating; how vulnerable I
am in my very connections.
Don't my worst anxieties rise out of just such ambiguous feelings of
communion and debt?

I'm suddenly swamped, overwhelmed in these tangles of unasked-for
    sympathies and alliances.
Always then, though, through an operation whose workings I'm never
    forced to explain to myself,
I'm released, the limits of my selfhood are reestablished, the nascent
    nightmare subsides,
and I'm able to reassume the not-incongruous sense of being alone and
    with so many others,
with nothing asked of me more than what any reasonable dream needs
    for its reasonable dreaming,
and the most minor qualms as to what I may have traded for my peace
    of mind, and what lost.

The Crime

Violence in the dream, violation of body and spirit; torment, mutilation,
      butchery, debasement.
At first it hardly feels real, there's something ceremonial in it, something
      of the dance.
The barbarisms seem formulaic, restrained, they cast a stillness about
      them, even a calm.
Then it comes once again, the torment, the debasement, and I have to
      accept that it's real.
Human beings are tearing each other to pieces, their rancor is real, and
      so is their pain.
Violence in the dream, but I still think—something wants me to think
      —there are *reasons*:
ideas are referred to, ideals, propositions of order, hierarchies, mores,
      structures of value.
Even in dream, though, I know it's not true, I know that if reasons there
      are, they're ill reasons.
Even in dream, I'm ashamed, and then, though I'm frightened, I steel
      myself and protest.
I protest, but the violence goes on, I cry out, but the pain, the rage, the
      rancor continue.
Then I suddenly realize I've said nothing at all, what I dreamed was
      spoken wasn't at all.
I dreamed I protested, I dreamed I cried out: I was mute, there was only
      an inarticulate moan.
What deceived me to think I'd objected when really I'd only cowered,
      embraced myself, moaned?
My incompetent courage deceived me, my too-timid hopes for the hu-
      man, my qualms, my doubts.
Besides the suspicion perhaps that the dream doesn't reveal the horror
      but draws it from itself,
that dream's truth is its violence, that its pity masks something I don't
      want to find there.

What I hear now in the dream is the dream lamenting, its sorrow, its
     fear, its cry.
Caught in the reasons of dream, I call out; caught in its sorrow, I know
     who I hear cry.

Shells

Shells of fearful insensitivity that I keep having to disadhere from my
      heart, how dream you?
How dream away these tireless reflexes of self-protection that almost define
      heart
and these sick startles of shame at confronting again the forms of fear the
      heart weaves,
the certitudes and the hatreds, the thoughtless fortifications of scarred,
      fearful self?
How dream you, heart hiding, how dream the products of heart foul
      with egotism and fear?
Heart's dream, the spaces holding you are so indistinct and the hurt place
      you lurk so tender,
that even in dream membranes veil and distort you, only fancy and
      falsehood hint where you are.
How can I dream the stripping away of the petrified membranes muffling
      the tremulous heart?
I reach towards the heart and attain only heart's stores of timidity, self-
      hatred, and blame;
the heart which I don't dare bring to my zone of knowledge for fear it
      will shame me again,
afflict me again with its pettiness, coyness, its sham zeal, false pity, and
      false pride.
Dream of my heart, am I only able to dream illusions of you that touch
      me with pity or pride?
How dream the heart's sorrow to redeem what it contains beyond its self-
      defense and disdain?
How forgive heart when the part of me that beholds heart swells so in
      its pride and contempt?
Trying to dream the dream of the heart, I hide myself from it, I veil my
      failures and shame.
Heart, ever unworthy of you, lost in you, will I ever truly dream you,
      or dream beyond you?

Room

I wanted to take up room. What a strange dream! I wanted to take up as
    much room as I could,
to swell up, enlarge, crowd into a corner all the others in the dream with
    me, but why?
Something to do with love, it felt like, but what love needs more volume
    than it has?
Lust, then: its limitlessness, the lure of its ineluctable renewal—but this
    came before lust.
Fear? Yes, the others were always more real than I was, more concrete,
    emphatic: why not fear?
Though I knew that this was my dream, they were the given and I the
    eccentric, wobbling variable.
A dubious plasma, drifting among them, self-consciously sidling, flowing,
    ebbing among them,
no wonder my atoms would boil, trying to gel, and no wonder I'd some-
    times resent them,
brood on them, trying to understand what they were, what my connection
    to them really was.
Sometimes I'd think the point of the dream was to find what of me was
    embodied in them.
What I was with them, though, what they finally were in themselves, I
    hardly could tell.
Sometimes they seemed beasts; I could see them only as beasts, captives
    of hunger and fear.
Sometimes they were angels, nearly on fire, embracing, gleaming with
    grace, gratitude, praise.
But when their lips touched, were they kissing, or gnawing the warmth
    from a maw?
So much threatening pain to each other, so much pain accomplished:
    no surprise I'd think beasts.
But still, I loved them; I wasn't just jealous of them, I loved them, was
    of them, and, more,
I'd grown somehow to know in the dream that part of my love meant
    accounting for them.

Account for them: how, though, why? Did they account for each other, would they for me?

That wasn't what the dream meant to be now; I loved them, I wasn't to ask if they loved me.

The fear, the loving and being loved, the accounting for and the wish to had all become one.

Dream, where have you brought me? What a strange dream! Who would have thought to be here?

Beasts, angels, taking up room, the ways of duty and love: what next, dream, where now?

History

I have escaped in the dream; I was in danger, at peril, at immediate,
    furious, frightening risk,
but I deftly evaded the risk, eluded the danger, I conned peril to think
    I'd gone that way,
then I went this, then this way again, over the bridges of innocence, into
    the haven of sorrow.
I was so shrewd in my moment of risk, so cool: I was as guileful as though
    I were guilty,
sly, devious, cunning, though I'd done nothing in truth but be who I
    was where I was
when the dream conceived me as a threat I wasn't, possessed of a power
    I'd never had,
though I had found enough strength to flee and the guileful wherewithal
    to elude and be free.
I have escaped and survived, but as soon as I think it it starts again, I'm
    hounded again:
no innocence now, no unlikeliest way, only this frenzied combing of the
    countries of mind
where I always believed I'd find safety and solace but where now are
    confusion and fear
and a turmoil so total that all I have known or might know drags me
    with it towards chaos.
That, in this space I inhabit, something fearsome is happening, headlong,
    with an awful momentum,
is never in doubt, but that's all I can say—no way even to be sure if I'm
    victim or oppressor;
absurd after all this not to know if I'm subject or object, scapegoat,
    perpetrator, or prey.
The dream is of beings like me, assembled, surrounded, herded like
    creatures, driven, undone.
And beings like me, not more like me but like me, assemble and herd
    them, us; undo us.
No escape now, no survival: captured, subjugated, undone, we all move
    through dreams of negation.

Subject, object, dream doesn't care; accumulate or subtract, self as solace, self-blame.

Thou shalt, thou shalt not; thus do I, thus I do not: dream is indifferent, bemused, abstracted.

Formulation, abstraction; assembly, removal: the dream detached; exaltation, execration, denial.

The Gap

So often and with such cruel fascination I have dreamed the implacable
    void that contains dream.
The space there, the silence, the scrawl of trajectories tracked, traced,
    and let go;
the speck of matter in non-matter; sphere, swing, the puff of agglutinate
    loose-woven tissue;
the endless pull of absence on self, the sad molecule of the self in its
    chunk of duration;
the desolate grain, flake, fragment of mind that thinks when the mind
    thinks it's thinking.
So often, too, with equal absorption, I have dreamed the end of it all:
    mind, matter, void.
I'm appalled, but I do it again, I dream it again, it comes uncalled for
    but it comes, always,
rising perhaps out of the fearful demands consciousness makes for linkage,
    coherence, congruence,
connection to something beyond, even if dread: mystery exponentially
    functioned to dread.
Again, premonitions of silence, the swoop through a gulf that might be
    inherent in mind
as though mind bore in its matter its own end and the annulment of
    everything else.
Somehow I always return in the dream from the end, from the mean-
    ingless, the mesh of despair,
but what if I don't once, what if the corrections fail once and I can't
    recover the thread
that leads back from that night beyond night that absorbs night as night
    absorbs innocent day?
The whole of being untempered by self, the great selves beyond self all
    wholly wound out;
sense neutered, knowledge betrayed: what if this is the real end of dream,
    facing the darkness
and subjecting the self yet again to imperious laws of doubt and denial
    which are never repealed?

How much can I do this, how often rejuvenate and redeem with such
partial, imperfect belief?
So often, by something like faith, I'm brought back in the dream; but
this, too; so often this, too.

The Knot

Deciphering and encoding, to translate, fabricate, revise; the abstract star,
    the real star;
crossing over boundaries we'd never known were there until we found
    ourselves beyond them.
A fascination first: this was why the dream existed, so our definitions
    would be realized.
Then more than fascination as we grasped how dream could infiltrate
    the mundane with its radiance.
There'd be no mundane anymore: wholly given to the dream, our de-
    bilitating skepticisms overcome,
we'd act, or would be acted on—the difference, if there'd been one,
    would have been annulled—
with such purity of motive and such temperate desire that outcome would
    result from inspiration
with the same illumination that the notion of creation brings when it
    first comes upon us.
No question now of fabricating less ambiguous futures, no trying to recast
    recalcitrant beginnings.
It would be another empire of determination, in which all movement
    would be movement towards—
mergings, joinings—and in which existence would be generated from
    the qualities of our volition:
intention flowing outward into form and back into itself in intricate
    threadings and weavings,
intuitions shaped as logically as crystal forms in rock, a linkage at the
    incandescent core,
knots of purpose we would touch into as surely as we touch the rippling
    lattice of a song.
No working out of what we used to call identity; our consummations
    would consist of acts,
of participating in a consciousness that wouldn't need, because it grew
    from such pure need,
acknowledgment or subject: we'd be held in it, always knowing there
    were truths beyond it.

Cleansed even of our appetite for bliss, we'd only want to know the
    ground of our new wonder,
and we wouldn't be surprised to find that it survived where we'd known
    it had to all along,
in all for which we'd blamed ourselves, repented and corrected, and never
    for a moment understood.

To Listen

In the dream of death where I listen, the voices of the dream keep
diminishing, fading away.
The dead are speaking, my dead are speaking, what they say seems urgent,
to me, to themselves,
but as I try to capture more clearly what I heard just moments ago, the
voices ebb and it's lost;
what's more, my impatience to know what was said seems to drive it
further out of my ken.
In the dream of death where I listen, I keep thinking my dead have a
message for me:
maybe they'll tell me at last why they must always die in the dream, live,
die, die again.
I still can't hear what they say, though; I force my senses into the silence
but nothing is there.
Sometimes I listen so hard I think what I'm waiting to hear must already
have been spoken,
it's here, its echo surrounds me, I just have to learn to bring it more
clearly within me
and I'll know at last what I never thought I would know about death and
the dead and the speech
of affection the dead speak that stays on in the sentient space between
living and after.
For the dead speak from affection, dream says, there's kindness in the
voices of the dead.
I listen again, but I still hear only fragments of the elaborate discourse
the dead speak;
when I try to capture its gist more is effaced, there are only faded words
strewn on the page
of my soul that won't rest from its need to have what it thinks it can have
from the dead.
Something is in me like greed now, I can't stop trying to tear the silence
away from the voices,
I tear at the actual voices, though I know what the dead bring us is not
to be held,

that the wanting to hold it is just what condemns dream to this pained,
    futile listening,
is what brings dream finally to its end, in silence, in want, in believing
    it's lost,
only for now, my dream thinks, at least let it be only for now, my forsaken
    dream thinks,
what the dead brought, what the dead found in their kind, blurred, weary
    voices to bring.

The Covenant

In my unlikeliest dream, my dead are with me again, companions again,
      in an ordinary way;
nothing of major moment to accomplish, no stains to cleanse, no oaths
      or debts to redeem:
my dead are serene, composed, as though they'd known all along how
      this would be.
Only I look aslant, only I brood and fret, marvel; only I have to know
      what this miracle is:
I'm awed, I want to embrace my newly found dead, to ask why they had
      to leave me so abruptly.
In truth, I think, I want pity from them, for my being bereft, for my
      grief and my pain.
But my dead will have none of my sorrow, of my asking how they came
      to be here again.
They anoint me with their mild regard and evidence only the need to
      continue, go on
in a dream that's almost like life in how only the plainest pastimes of
      love accumulate worth.
Cured of all but their presence, they seem only to want me to grasp their
      new way of being.
At first I feel nothing, then to my wonder and perhaps, too, the wonder
      of the dead,
I sense an absence in them, of will, of anything like will, as though will
      in the soul
had for the dead been all given over, transfigured, to humility, resig-
      nation, submission.
I know without knowing how that the dead can remember the movements
      of will, thought willing,
the gaze fixed at a distance that doesn't exist, the mind in its endless war
      with itself—
those old cravings—but the striving to will themselves from themselves
      is only a dream,
the dead know what death has brought is all they need now because all
      else was already possessed,

all else was a part of the heart as it lived, in what it had seen and what
it had suffered,
in the love it had hardly remarked coming upon it, so taken it was with
its work of volition.
I can hardly believe that so little has to be lost to find such good fortune
in death,
and then, as I dream again the suspensions of will I'm still only just able
to dream,
I suddenly know I've beheld death myself, and instead of the terror, the
flexions of fear,
the repulsion, recoil, impatience to finish, be done with the waiting once
and for all,
I feel the same surge of acceptance, patience, and joy I felt in my dead
rising in me:
I know that my dead have brought what I've restlessly waited all the life
of the dream for.
I wait in joy as they give themselves to the dream once again; waiting,
I'm with them again.

Helen

1

More voice was in her cough tonight: its first harsh, stripping sound
    would weaken abruptly,
and he'd hear the voice again, not hers, unrecognizable, its notes from
    somewhere else,
someone saying something they didn't seem to want to say, in a tongue
    they hadn't mastered,
or a singer, diffident and hesitating, searching for a place to start an
    unfamiliar melody.

Its pitch was gentle, almost an interrogation, intimate, a plea, a moan,
    almost sexual,
but he could hear assertion, too, a straining from beneath, a forcing at
    the withheld consonant,
and he realized that she was holding back, trying with great effort not to
    cough again,
to change the spasm to a tone instead and so avert the pain that lurked
    out at the stress.

Then he heard her lose her almost-word, almost-song: it became a groan,
    the groan a gasp,
the gasp a sigh of desperation, then the cough rasped everything away,
    everything was cough now,
he could hear her shuddering, the voice that for a moment seemed the
    gentlest part of her,
choked down, effaced, abraded, taken back, as all of her was being taken
    from him now.

2

In the morning she was standing at the window; he lay where he was
    and quietly watched her.

A sound echoed in from somewhere, she turned to listen, and he was
      shocked at how she moved:
not *enough* moved, just her head, pivoting methodically, the mechanisms
      slowed nearly to a halt,
as though she was afraid to jar herself with the contracting tendons and
      skeletal leverings.

A flat, cool, dawn light washed in on her: how pale her skin was, how
      dull her tangled hair.
So much of her had burned away, and what was left seemed draped
      listlessly upon her frame.
It was her eye that shocked him most, though; he could only see her
      profile, and the eye in it,
without fire or luster, was strangely isolated from her face, and even from
      her character.

For the time he looked at her, the eye existed not as her eye, his wife's,
      his beloved's eye,
but as *an* eye, an object, so emphatic, so pronounced, it was separate
      both from what it saw
and from who saw with it: it could have been a creature's eye, a member
      of that larger class
which simply indicated sight and not that essence which her glance had
      always brought him.

It came to him that though she hadn't given any sign, she knew that he
      was watching her.
He was saddened that she'd tolerate his seeing her as she was now, weak,
      disheveled, haggard.
He felt that they were both involved, him watching, her letting him, in
      a depressing indiscretion:
she'd always, after all their time together, only offered him the images
      she thought he wanted.

She'd known how much he needed beauty, how much presumed it as
      the elemental of desire.
The loveliness that illuminated her had been an engrossing narrative his
      spirit fed on;

he entered it and flowed out again renewed for having touched within
    and been a part of it.
In his meditations on her, he'd become more complicated, fuller, more
    essential to himself.

It was to her beauty he'd made love at first, she was there within its
    captivating light,
but was almost secondary, as though she was just the instance of some
    overwhelming generality.
She herself was shy before it; she, too, as unassumingly as possible was
    testing this abstraction
which had taken both of them into its sphere, rendering both subservient
    to its serene enormity.

As their experience grew franker, and as she learned to move more
    confidently towards her core,
became more overtly active in elaborating needs and urges, her beauty
    still came first.
In his memory, it seemed to him that they'd unsheathed her from the
    hazes of their awe,
as though her unfamiliar, fiery, famished nakedness had been disclosed
    as much to her as him.

She'd been grateful to him, and that gratitude became in turn another
    fact of his desire.
Her beauty had acknowledged him, allowed him in its secret precincts,
    let him be its celebrant,
an implement of its luxurious materiality, and though he remained as-
    tonished by it always,
he fulfilled the tasks it demanded of him, his devotions reinvigorated and
    renewed.

3

In the deepest sense, though, he'd never understood what her beauty was
    or really meant.
If you only casually beheld her, there were no fanfares, you were taken
    by no immolating ecstasies.

It amused him sometimes seeing other men at first not really understand-
ing what they saw;
no one dared to say it, but he could feel them holding back their dis-
appointment or disbelief.

Was this Helen, mythic Helen, this female, fleshed like any other, im-
perfect and approachable?
He could understand: he himself, when he'd first seen her, hadn't really;
he'd even thought,
before he'd registered her spirit and intelligence, before her laughter's
melodies had startled him—
if only one could alter such and such, improve on this or that: he hardly
could believe it now.

But so often he'd watched others hear her speak, or laugh, look at her
again, and fall in love,
as puzzled as he'd been at the time they'd wasted while their raptures of
enchantment took.
Those who hadn't ever known her sometimes spoke of her as though she
were his thing, his toy,
but that implied something static in her beauty, and she was surely just
the opposite of that.

If there was little he'd been able to explain of what so wonderfully absorbed
him in her,
he knew it was a movement and a process, that he was taken towards
and through her beauty,
touched by it but even more participating in its multiplicities, the rev-
elations of its grace.
He felt himself becoming real in her, tangible, as though before he'd
only half existed.

Sometimes he would even feel it wasn't really him being brought to such
unlikely fruition.
Absurd that anyone so coarse and ordinary should be in touch with such
essential mystery:
something else, beyond him, something he would never understand,
used him for its affirmations.

What his reflections came to was something like humility, then a gratitude
of his own.

4

The next night her cough was worse, with a harsher texture, the spasms
came more rapidly,
and they'd end with a deep, complicated emptying, like the whining
flattening of a bagpipe.
The whole event seemed to need more labor: each cough sounded more
futile than the last,
as though the effort she'd made and the time lost making it had added
to the burden of illness.

Should he go to her? He felt she'd moved away from him, turning more
intently towards herself.
Her sickness absorbed her like a childbirth; she seemed almost like some-
one he didn't know.
There'd been so many Helens, the first timid girl, then the sensual Helen
of their years together,
then the last, whose grace had been more intricate and difficult to know
and to exult in.

How childishly frightened he'd always been by beauty's absence, by its
destruction or perversity.
For so long he let himself be tormented by what he knew would have to
happen to her.
He'd seen the old women as their thighs and buttocks bloated, then
withered and went slack,
as their dugs dried, skin dried, legs were sausaged with the veins that rose
like kelp.

He'd tried to overcome himself, to feel compassion towards them, but,
perhaps because of her,
he'd felt only a shameful irritation, as though they were colluding in
their loss.
Whether they accepted what befell them, even, he would think, gladly
acquiescing to it,

or fought it, with all their sad and valiant unguents, dyes, and ointments, was equally degrading.

His own body had long ago become a ruin, but beauty had never been a part of what he was.
What would happen to his lust, and to his love, when time came to savage and despoil her?
He already felt his will deserting him; for a long time, though, nothing touched or dulled her:
perhaps she really was immortal, maybe his devotion kept her from the steely rakings of duration.

Then, one day, something at her jowls; one day her hips; one day the flesh at her elbows . . .
One day, one day, one day he looked at her and knew that what he'd feared so was upon them.
He couldn't understand how all his worst imaginings had come to pass without his noticing.
Had he all this while been blind, or had he not wanted to acknowledge what he'd dreaded?

He'd been gazing at her then; in her wise way, she'd looked back at him, and touched him,
and he knew she'd long known what was going on in him: another admiration took him,
then another fire, and that simply, he felt himself closer to her: there'd been no trial,
nothing had been lost, of lust, of love, and something he'd never dreamed would be was gained.

5

With her in the darkness now, not even touching her, he sensed her fever's suffocating dryness.
He couldn't, however much he wanted to, not let himself believe she was to be no more.
And there was nothing he could do for her even if she'd let him; he tried to calm himself.

Her cough was hollow, soft, almost forgiving, ebbing slowly through the
   volumes of her thorax.

He could almost hear that world as though from in her flesh: the current
   of her breath,
then her breastbone, ribs, and spine, taking on the cough's vibrations,
   giving back their own.
Then he knew precisely how she was within herself as well, he was with
   her as he'd never been:
he'd unmoored in her, cast himself into the night of her, and perceived
   her life with her.

All she'd lived through, all she'd been and done, he could feel accu-
   mulated in this instant.
The impressions and sensations, feelings, dreams, and memories were
   tearing loose in her,
had disconnected from each other and randomly begun to float, collide,
   collapse, entangle;
they were boiling in a matrix of sheer chance, suspended in a purely
   mental universe of possibility.

He knew that what she was now to herself, what she remembered, might
   not in truth have ever been.
Who, then, was she now, who was the person she had been, if all she
   was, all he still so adored,
was muddled, addled, mangled: what of her could be repository now,
   the place where she existed?
When everything was shorn from her, what within this flux of fragments
   still stayed her?

He knew then what he had to do: he was so much of her now and she
   of him that she was his,
her consciousness and memory both his, he would will her into him,
   keep her from her dissolution.
All the wreckage of her fading life, its shattered hours taken in this fearful
   flood,
its moments unrecoverable leaves twirling in a gust across a waste of loss,
   he drew into himself,

and held her, kept her, all the person she had been was there within his
sorrow and his longing:
it didn't matter what delirium had captured her, what of her was being
lacerated, rent,
his pain had taken on a power, his need for her became a force that he
could focus on her;
there was something in him like triumph as he shielded her within the
absolute of his affection.

Then he couldn't hold it, couldn't keep it, it was all illusion, a confection
of his sorrow:
there wasn't room within the lenses of his mortal being to contain what
she had been,
to do justice to a single actual instant of her life and soul, a single moment
of her mind,
and he released her then, let go of this diminished apparition he'd created
from his fear.

But still, he gave himself to her, without moving moved to her: she was
still his place of peace.
He listened for her breath: was she still here with him, did he have her
that way, too?
He heard only the flow of the silent darkness, but he knew now that in
it they'd become it,
their shells of flesh and form, the old delusion of their separateness and
incompletion, gone.

When one last time he tried to bring her image back, she was as vivid
as he'd ever seen her.
What they were together, everything they'd lived, all that seemed so
fragile, bound in time,
had come together in him, in both of them: she had entered death, he
was with her in it.
Death was theirs, she'd become herself again; her final, searing loveliness
had been revealed.

New Poems

Secrets

I didn't know the burly old man who lived in a small house like ours
     down the block in Newark
was a high-up in the mob on the docks until I was grown and my father
     told me about him.

I didn't know until much too much later that my superior that year in
     the stockroom at Nisner's,
a dazzlingly bright black man, would never in those days climb out of
     his airless, monotonous cellar.

Neither did I know that the club where I danced every night in Philly
     in the early seventies—
it was almost my home—was controlled by loan sharks and infested by
     addicts and cokeheads.

The councilman on the take, the grocer-gambler, the blond girl upstairs
     giving free oral sex—
it was all news to me: do people hide things from me to protect me? Do
     they mistrust me?

Even when Sid Mizraki was found beaten to death in an alley, I didn't
     hear till years later,
Sid murdered! Oh, god, my god, was all I could say: poor, sad Sid, poor
     hard-luck Sidney!

I didn't know Sidney that well, but I liked him: plump, awkward, he was
     gentle, eager to please,
the way unprepossessing people will be; we played ball, went to China-
     town with the guys.

He'd had a bleak life: childhood in the streets, bad education, no women,
     irrelevant jobs;
when I knew him he worked for the city, then stopped; I had no idea of
     his true tribulations.

As the tale finally found me, Sid had a boss who hated him, rode him, drove him insane,
and Sid one drunk night in a bar bribed some burglars he knew to kill the creep for him.

I can't conceive how you'd dream up something like that, or how you'd know people like that,
but apparently Sid had access to tax rolls, and rich people's addresses he was willing to trade.

Then suddenly he was transferred, got a friendlier boss, forgot the whole witless affair,
but a year or so later the thieves were caught and as part of their plea bargain sold Sid.

Sid got off with probation, but was fired, of course, and who'd hire him with that record?
He worked as a bartender, went on relief, drifted, got into drugs, some small-time dealing.

Then he got married—"to the plainest woman on earth," someone told me—but soon divorced:
more drugs, more dealing, run-ins with cops, then his unthinkable calvary in that alley.

It was never established who did it, or why; no one but me was surprised it had happened.
A bum found him, bleeding, broken, inert; a friend from before said, "His torments are over."

So, Sidney, what now? Shall I sing for you, celebrate you with some truth? Here's truth:
add up what you didn't know, poor friend, and I don't, and you might have one conscious person.

No, this has nothing to do with your omissions or sins or failed rectifications, but mine:

to come so close to a life and not comprehend it, acknowledge it, truly
 know it is life.

How can I feel so clearly the shudder of blows, even the blessed oblivion
 breaking on you,
and not really grasp what you were in yourself to yourself, what secrets
 sustained you?

So maybe if anyone's soul should be singing, it's yours; I think I know
 what you'd tell me:
Poor sensitive, sheltered creature; poor poet: if you can't open your eyes,
 at least be still.

Hercules, Deianira, Nessus

from Ovid, Metamorphoses, *Book IX*

There was absolutely no reason after the centaur had pawed her and tried
    to mount her,
after Hercules waiting across the raging river for the creature to carry her
    to him
heard her cry out and launched an arrow soaked in the Hydra's incurable
    venom into the monster,
that Deianira should have believed him, Nessus, horrible thing, as he
    died but she did.

We see the end of the story: Deianira anguished, aghast, suicide-sword
    in her hand;
Hercules' blood hissing and seething like water into which molten rods
    are plunged to anneal,
but how could a just-married girl hardly out of her father's house have
    envisioned all that,
and even conjecturing that Nessus was lying, plotting revenge, how could
    she have been sure?

We see the centaur as cunning, malignant, a hybrid from the savage
    time before ours
when emotion always was passion and passion was always unchecked by
    commandment or conscience;
she sees only a man-horse, mortally hurt, suddenly harmless, eyes sud-
    denly soft as a foal's,
telling her, "Don't be afraid, come closer, listen": offering homage,
    friendship, a favor.

In our age of scrutiny and dissection we know Deianira's mind better
    than she does herself:
we know the fortune of women as chattel and quarry, objects to be won
    then shunted aside;
we understand the cost of repression, the repercussions of unsatisfied rage
    and resentment,

but consciousness then was still new, Deianira inhabited hers like the
    light from a fire.

Or might she have glimpsed with that mantic prescience the gods hadn't
    taken away yet
her hero a lifetime later on the way home with another king's daughter,
    callow, but lovely,
lovely enough to erase from Hercules' scruples not only his vows but the
    simple convention
that tells you you don't bring a rival into your aging wife's weary, sorrowful
    bed?

. . . No, more likely the centaur's promise intrigued in itself: an infallible
    potion of love.
"Just gather the clots of blood from my wound: here, use my shirt, then
    hide it away.
Though so exalted, so regal a woman as you never would need it, it
    might still be of use:
whoever's shoulders it touches, no matter when, will helplessly, hope-
    lessly love you forever."

See Hercules now in the shirt Deianira has sent him approaching the
    fires of an altar,
the garment suddenly clinging, the Hydra, his long-vanquished foe, alive
    in its threads,
each thread a tentacle clutching at him, each chemical tentacle acid,
    adhering, consuming,
charring before his horrified eyes skin from muscle, muscle from tendon,
    tendon from bone.

Now Deianira, back then, the viscous gouts of Nessus's blood dyeing her
    diffident hands:
if she could imagine us watching her there in her myth, how would she
    want us to see her?
Surely as symbol, a petal of sympathy caught in the perilous rift between
    culture and chaos,
not as the nightmare she'd be, a corpse with a slash of tardy self-knowledge
    deep in its side.

What Hercules sees as he pounds up the bank isn't himself cremated
      alive on his pyre,
shrieking as Jove his Olympian father extracts his immortal essence from
      its agonized sheathing—
he sees what's before him: the woman, his bride, kneeling to the dark,
      rushing river,
obsessively scrubbing away, he must think, the nocuous, mingled reek
      of horse, Hydra, human.

Instinct

Although he's apparently the youngest (his little rasta-beard is barely down
     and feathers),

most casually connected (he hardly glances at the girl he's with, though
     she might be his wife),

half-sloshed (or more than half) on picnic-whiskey teen-aged father, when
     his little son,

two or so, tumbles from the slide, hard enough to scare himself, hard
     enough to make him cry,

really cry, not partly cry, not pretend the fright for what must be some
     scarce attention,

but really let it out, let loudly be revealed the fear of having been so
     close to real fear,

he, the father, knows just how quickly he should pick the child up, then
     how firmly hold it,

fit its head into the muscled socket of his shoulder, rub its back, croon
     and whisper to it,

and finally pull away a little, about a head's length, looking, still con-
     cerned, into its eyes,

then smiling, broadly, brightly, as though something had been shared,
     something of importance,

not dreadful, or not very, not at least now that it's past, but rather
     something . . . funny,

funny, yes, it was funny, wasn't it, to fall and cry like that, though one
     certainly can understand,

we've all had glimpses of a premonition of the anguish out there, you're
     better now, though,

aren't you, why don't you go back and try again, I'll watch you, maybe
     have another drink,

yes, my son, my love, I'll go back and be myself now! You go be the
     person you are, too.

Dominion: Depression

I don't know what day or year of their secret cycle this blazing golden
    afternoon might be,
but out in the field in a shrub hundreds of pairs of locusts are locked in
    a slow sexual seizure.

Hardly more animate than the few leaves they haven't devoured, they
    seethe like a single being,
limbs, antennas, and wings all tangled together as intricately as a layer
    of neurons.

Always the neat, tight, gazeless helmet, the exoskeleton burnished like
    half-hardened glue;
always the abdomen twitched deftly under or aside, the skilled rider, the
    skillfully ridden.

One male, though, has somehow severed a log, it sways on the spike of
    a twig like a harp:
he lunges after his female, tilts, falls; the mass horribly shudders, shifts,
    realigns.

So dense, so hard, so immersed in their terrible need to endure, so unlike
    me but like me,
why do they seem such a denial, why do I feel if I plunged my hand in
    among them I'd die?

This must be what god thinks beholding his ignorant, obstinate, libidi-
    nally maniacal offspring:
wanting to stop them, to keep them from being so much an image of
    his impotence or his will.

How divided he is from his creation: even here near the end he sees
    moving towards him
a smaller, sharper, still more gleaming something, extracting moist matter
    from a skull.

No more now: he waits, his fists full of that mute, oily, crackling, crys-
talline broil,
then he feels at last the cool wingbeat of the innocent void moving in
again over the world.

My Fly

for Erving Goffman, 1922–82

One of those great, garishly emerald flies that always look freshly generated
      from fresh excrement
and who maneuver through our airspace with a deft intentionality that
      makes them seem to think,
materializes just above my desk, then vanishes, his dense, abrasive buzz
      sucked in after him.

I wait, imagine him, hidden somewhere, waiting, too, then think, who
      knows why, of you—
don't laugh—that he's a messenger from you, or that you yourself (you'd
      howl at this),
ten years afterwards have let yourself be incarnated as this pestering anti-
      angel.

Now he, or you, abruptly reappears, with a weightless pounce alighting
      near my hand.
I lean down close, and though he has to sense my looming presence, he
      patiently attends,
as though my study of him had become an element of his own
      observations—maybe it is you!

Joy! To be together, even for a time! Yes, tilt your fuselage, turn it towards
      the light,
aim the thousand lenses of your eyes back up at me: how I've missed the
      layers of your attention,
how often been bereft without your gift for sniffing out pretentiousness
      and moral sham.

Why would you come back, though? Was that other radiance not intricate
      enough to parse?
Did you find yourself in some monotonous century hovering down the
      tidy queue of creatures
waiting to experience again the eternally unlikely bliss of being matter
      and extension?

You lift, you land—you're rushed, I know; the interval in all our terminals
    is much too short.
Now you hurl against the window, skid and jitter on the pane: I open it
    and step aside
and follow for one final moment of felicity your brilliant, ardent atom
    swerving through.

Spider Psyche

The mummified spider hung in its own web in the rafters striped legs
    coiled tightly
into its body head hunched a bit into what would be shoulders if it had
    been human
indicating a knowledge perhaps of the death coming to take it indicating
    not fear of death
I surmise but an emotion like wanting to be ready or ready on time trying
    to prepare psyche
for death so psyche won't fall back into the now useless brain the core
    imprinted with all
it knew in the world until now but only a nub now no longer receptor
    receptacle rather
and perhaps psyche did it didn't flinch rather just gazed out of the web
    of perception
watching the wave of not-here take the shore-edge of here acknowledging
    rather its portion
of being the blare of light in the corner the grain in the wood the old
    odors and the space
a great cup underneath a great gaping under the breadth of your being
    so that you want
no matter what this last moment of holding even if shoulders and brain
    can hardly abide it
even if brain swoons nearly trying to hold its last thought last fusion of
    will and cognition
and there is no end in this ending no contingent condition of being this
    glare of perception
hurl of sensation all one sense and intention act and love my psyche my
    spider love and hope
take us dear spider of self into your otherness into having once been and
    the knowledge of having
in all this been once in wonder so every instant was thanks and all else
    was beneath and adrift
my spider-psyche all awe now all we ever wanted to be now in this great
    gratitude gone

Time: 1976

1

Time for my break; I'm walking from my study down the long hallway
  towards the living room.
Catherine is there, on the couch, reading to Jed, the phonograph is
  playing Bach's *Offering*.
I can just hear Catherine's voice as she shows Jed the pictures: *Voilà le
  château, voilà Babar,*
and with no warning I'm taken with a feeling that against all logic I
  recognize to be regret,
as violent and rending a regret as anything I've ever felt, and I understand
  immediately
that all of this familiar beating and blurring, the quickening breath, the
  gathering despair,
almost painful all, has to do with the moment I'm in, and my mind,
  racing to keep order,
thrusts this way and that and finally casts itself, my breath along with it,
  into the future.

2

Ten years from now, or twenty: I'm walking down the same hallway, I
  hear the same music,
the same sounds—Catherine's story, Jed's chirps of response—but I know
  with anxiety
that most of this is only in my mind: the reality is that Catherine and
  Jed are no longer there,
that I'm merely constructing this—what actually accompanies me down
  that corridor is memory:
here, in this tentative but terribly convincing future I think to myself that
  it must be the music—
the Bach surely is real, I can *hear* it—that drives me so poignantly,
  expectantly back

to remember again that morning of innocent peace a lifetime ago when
I came towards them;
the sunny room, the music, the voices, each more distinct now: *Voilà
le château, voilà Babar* . . .

3

But if I'm torn so with remembrance in *this* present, then something
here must be lost.
Has Jed grown, already left home? Has Catherine gone on somewhere,
too, to some other life?
But no, who'd have played the record: perhaps they, or one of them,
either one would be enough,
will still be out there before me, not speaking, perhaps reading, looking
out the window, waiting.
Maybe all this grief, then, was illusion; a sadness, not for loss, but for
the nature of time:
in my already fading future, I try to find a reconciliation for one more
imaginary loss . . .
All this, sensation, anxiety, and speculation, goes through me in an
instant, then in another,
a helplessness at what mind will do, then back into the world: *Voilà
Babar, voilà la vieille dame* . . .

Time: 1978

1

What could be more endearing, on a long, too quiet, lonely evening in
     an unfamiliar house,
than, on the table before us, Jed's sneakers, which, finally, at eleven
     o'clock, I notice,
tipped on their sides, still tied, the soles barely scuffed since we just
     bought them today,
or rather submitted to Jed's picking them out, to his absolutely having
     to have them,
the least practical pair, but the first thing besides toys he's ever cared so
     much about,
and which, despite their impossible laces and horrible color, he passion-
     ately wanted, *desired*,
and coerced us into buying, by, when we made him try on the sensible
     pair we'd chosen,
limping in them, face twisted in torment: his first experience of anguish
     at a violated aesthetic.

2

What more endearing except Jed himself, who, now, perhaps because
     of the new night noises,
wakes, and, not saying a word, pads in to sit on Catherine's lap, head
     on her breast, silent,
only his breathing, sleep-quickened, as I write this, trying to get it all in,
     hold the moments
between the sad desolation I thought if not to avert then to diminish in
     writing it down,
and this, now, my pen scratching, eyes rushing to follow the line and
     not lose Jed's gaze,
which dims with sleep now, wanders to the window—hill, oak, field cleft
     with trenches—

and begins to flutter so that I can't keep up with it: quick, quick, before
    you're asleep,
listen, how and whenever if not now, right now, will I speak to you,
    both of you, of all this?

Interrogation II

after the painting by Leon Golub

(Four interrogators; a victim, bound and hooded; red walls,
a ladderlike device with chain; a chair)

1

There will always be an issue: doctrine, dogma, differences of conscience,
    politics, or creed.
There will always be a reason: heresy, rebellion, dissidence, inadequate
    conviction, or compliance.

There will always be the person to command it: president or king, dictator
    or chief of staff,
and the priest or parson to anoint it, consecrate it, bless it, ground its
    logic in the sacred.

There will always be the victim; trembling, fainting, fearful, abducted,
    bound, and brought here;
there will always be the order, and the brutes, thugs, reptiles, scum, to
    carry out the order.

There will always be the room, the chair, the room whose walls are
    blood, the chair of shame.
There will always be the body, hooded, helpless; and the soul within,
    trembling, fearful, shamed.

2

If I am here, hooded, helpless,
within these walls of blood,

upon this chair of shame,
something had to think me here.

I lived within my life,
I only thought my life,

I was stolen from it:
something *thought* me from it.

If something thought me,
there had to be a mind,

and if there was a mind,
it had to be contained, revealed,

as I thought mine was contained,
within a strip of temporal being.

If it was another mind,
like mine, that thought

and bound and brought me here,
some other consciousness

within its strip of being,
didn't it, that bit of being,

have to feel as I must feel
the nothingness against it,

the nothingness encroaching
on the rind of temporality,

the strand of actuality,
in which it is revealed?

Wasn't it afraid
to jeopardize the sensitivity

with which it knows itself,
with which it senses being

trembling upon nothingness,
struggling against nothingness,

with which it holds away
the nothingness within itself

which seems to strive to join
into that greater void?

When it stole me from my life,
abducted me and bound me,

wouldn't it have felt itself
being lost within the void

of nothingness within it?
Wasn't it afraid?

3

Why are you crying?
Nothing is happening.

No one is being tortured,
no one beaten.

Why are you crying?
Nothing is happening.

No one's genitals nails spine
crushed torn out shattered.

No one's eardrums burst with fists,
no one's brain burst with bludgeons.

Why are you crying?
Nothing is happening.

No one's bones unsocketed
fractured leaching marrow.

No one flayed, flogged, maimed,
seared with torches,

set afire racked
shot electrocuted hung.

Why are you crying?
Nothing is happening.

There is only a chair,
a room, a ladder,

flesh indelibly marked
with pain and shame.

Why are you crying?
Nothing is happening.

4

The human soul, the soul
we share, the single soul,

that by definition
which is our essential being,

is composed of other souls,
inhabited by other beings:

thus its undeniable power,
its purity, its vision,

thus its multiplicity
in singularity.

I understand the composition
of the soul, its communality,

but must I share my soul
with brutes and reptiles,

must I share my being,
vision, purity with scum?

Impossible that in the soul
the human species

should be represented
as these brutes and thugs;

mortal substance
bodied as these reptiles.

Soul would loathe itself,
detest its very substance,

huddle in its lurk of essence
howling out its grief

of temporality, snarling out
its rage of mutability,

rather than be represented
by these beasts of prey.

The human soul is being
devoured by beasts of prey.

The human soul is prey.

5

I didn't know the ladder to divinity on which were dreamed ascending
    and descending angels,
on which sodden spirit was supposed to rarify and rise, had become an
    instrument of torment,
wrist-holes punctured in its rungs, chains to hold the helpless body ham-
    mered in its uprights.

I didn't know how incidental life can seem beside such implements of
    pain and degradation;
neither did I know, though, how much presence can be manifested in
    the hooded, helpless body:
brutalized and bound, sinews, muscles, skin, still are lit with grace and
    pride and hope.

We cry from shame, because the body and the soul within are mocked,
    displayed, and shamed.
There will always be a reason, there will always be a victim, rooms of
    blood, chairs of pain.
But will there be the presence, grace and hope and pride enduring past
    the pain and shame?

The Game

"Water" was her answer and I fell instantly and I knew self-destructively
    in love with her,
had to have her, would, I knew, someday, I didn't care how, and soon,
    too, have her,
though I guessed already it would have to end badly though not so
    disastrously as it did.

My answer, "lion" or "eagle," wasn't important: the truth would have
    been anything but myself.
The game of that first fateful evening was what you'd want to come back
    as after you died;
it wasn't the last life-or-death contest we'd have, only the least erotically
    driven and dangerous.

What difference if she was married, and perhaps mad (both only a little,
    I thought wrongly)?
There was only my jealous glimpse of her genius, then my vision of
    vengeance: midnight, morning—
beneath me a planet possessed: cycles of transfiguration and soaring,
    storms crossing.

My Book, My Book

The book goes fluttering crazily through the space of my room toward
     the wall like a bird
stunned in mid-flight and impacts and falls not like a bird but more
     brutally, like a man,
mortally sprawling, spine torn from its sutures, skeletal glue fragmented
     to crystal and dust.

Numb, submissive, inert, it doesn't as would any other thing wounded
     shudder, quake, shiver,
act out at least desperate, reflexive attempts toward persistence, endur-
     ance, but how could it,
wasn't it shriven already of all but ambition and greed; rote, lame em-
     ulations of conviction?

. . . Arrives now to my mind the creature who'll sniff out someday what
     in this block of pretension,
what protein, what atom, might still remain to digest and abstract, trans-
     figure to gist,
what trace of life-substance wasn't abraded away by the weight of its
     lovelessness and its sham.

Come, little borer, sting your way in, tunnel more deeply, blast, mine,
     excavate, drill:
take my book to you, etherealize me in the crunch of your gut; refine
     me, release me;
let me cling to your brain stem, dissolve in your dreaming: verse, page,
     quire; devour me, devourer.

Villanelle of the Suicide's Mother

Sometimes I almost go hours without crying,
Then I feel if I don't, I'll go insane.
It can seem her whole life was her dying.

She tried so hard, then she was tired of trying;
Now I'm tired, too, of trying to explain.
Sometimes I almost go hours without crying.

The anxiety, the rage, the denying;
Though I never blamed her for my pain,
It can seem her whole life was her dying,

And mine was struggling to save her: prying,
Conniving: it was the chemistry in her brain.
Sometimes I almost go hours without crying.

If I said she was easy, I'd be lying;
The lens between her and the world was stained:
It can seem her whole life was her dying

But the fact, the *fact*, is stupefying:
Her absence tears at me like a chain.
Sometimes I almost go hours without crying.
It can seem her whole life was her dying.

Thirst

Here was my relation with the woman who lived all last autumn and
winter day and night
on a bench in the Hundred and Third Street subway station until finally
one day she vanished:

we regarded each other, scrutinized one another: me shyly, obliquely,
trying not to be furtive;
she boldly, unblinkingly, even pugnaciously; wrathfully even, when her
bottle was empty.

I was frightened of her, I felt like a child, I was afraid some repressed
part of myself
would go out of control and I'd be forever entrapped in the shocking
seethe of her stench.

Not excrement, merely, not merely surface and orifice going unwashed,
rediffusion of rum:
there was will in it, and intention, power and purpose; a social, ethical
rage and rebellion.

. . . Despair, too, though, grief, loss: sometimes I'd think I should take
her home with me,
bathe her, comfort her, dress her: she wouldn't have wanted me to, I
would think.

Instead I'd step into my train: how rich, I would think, is the lexicon of
our self-absolving;
how insane our bland, fatal assurance that reflection is righteousness
being accomplished.

The dance of our glances, the clash: pulling each other through our
perceptual punctures;
then holocaust, holocaust: host on host of ill, injured presences squan-
dered, consumed.

Her vigil, somewhere, I know, continues: her occupancy, her absolute,
     faithful attendance;
the dance of our glances: challenge, abdication, effacement; the perfume
     of our consternation.

Index of Titles

Index of First Lines

Did I write this, 41

do you remember learning to tie your shoes?, 28

Doesn't, when we touch it, that sheen of infinitesimally pebbled steel, doesn't it, perhaps, 128

Each movement of the Mozart has a soloist and as each appears the conductor tunes her instrument,
144

Even here, in a forest in the foothills of a range of mountains, lucent air, the purest dawn, 198

Except for the dog, that she wouldn't have him put away, wouldn't let him die, I'd have liked her,
86

Except for the little girl, 9

Except for the undeniable flash of envy I feel, the reflexive competitiveness, he's inconsequential,
174

He drives, she mostly sleeps; when she's awake, they quarrel, and now, in a violet dusk, 166

He hasn't taken his eyes off you since we walked in, although you seem not to notice particularly,
219

He was very much the less attractive of the two: heavyset, part punk, part L. L. Bean, 176

He'd been a clod, he knew, yes, always aiming toward his vision of the good life, always acting on
it, 126

Here was my relation with the woman who lived all last autumn and winter day and night, 278

He's not sure how to get the jack on—he must have recently bought the car, although it's an
ancient, 171

How well I have repressed the dream of death I had after the war when I was nine in Newark, 169

I am afraid for you a little, for your sense of shame; I feel you are accustomed to ordinary evil, 133

I am going to rip myself down the middle into two pieces, 23

I didn't know the burly old man who lived in a small house like ours down the block in Newark,
253

I don't know what day or year of their secret cycle this blazing golden afternoon might be, 260

I feel terribly strong today, 31

I have escaped in the dream; I was in danger, at peril, at immediate, furious, frightening risk, 233

I have found what pleases my friend's chubby, rosy, gloriously shining-eyed year-old daughter, 88

I hook my fingers into the old tennis court fence, 16

I know, 41

I look onto an alley here, 3

I sit in my room, 37

I think most people are relieved the first time they actually know someone who goes crazy, 62

"I want," he says again, through his tears, in this unfamiliar voice, again, "I want, I want," 177

I wanted to take up room. What a strange dream! I wanted to take up as much room as I could,
231

I'd like every girl in the world to have a poem of her own, 32

If you put in enough hours in bars, sooner or later you get to hear every imaginable kind of bullshit,
55

I'm on my way to the doctor to get the result of chest X-rays because I coughed blood, 164